MEMORIES *of* ME

A COMPLETE GUIDE TO TELLING
AND SHARING THE STORIES OF YOUR LIFE

MEMORIES *of* ME

A COMPLETE GUIDE TO TELLING AND SHARING THE STORIES OF YOUR LIFE

LAURA HEDGECOCK

PLAIN SIGHT PUBLISHING
AN IMPRINT OF CEDAR FORT, INC.
SPRINGVILLE, UTAH

ISBN 13: 978-1-4621-1453-5

Published by Plain Sight Publications, an imprint of Cedar Fort, Inc.
2373 W. 700 S., Springville, UT 84663
Distributed by Cedar Fort, Inc., www.cedarfort.com

Library of Congress Cataloging-in-Publication Data

Hedgecock, Laura, 1961- author.
 Memories of me : a complete guide to telling and sharing the stories of your life / Laura Hedgecock.
    pages cm
 Includes bibliographical references and index.
 ISBN 978-1-4621-1453-5 (alk. paper)
 1. Autobiography--Authorship. I. Title.

CT25.H43 2014
808.06'692--dc23

2014002461

Cover design by Angela D. Baxter
Cover design © 2014 by Lyle Mortimer
Edited and typeset by Daniel Friend

Printed in the United States of America

10 9 8 7 6 5 4 3 2 1

Printed on acid-free paper

*In memory of Hazel Savoy Crymes,
who taught us all how to treasure life.*

CONTENTS

Note: Worksheets and Writing Excercises can be printed out at cedarfort. com/memories.

INTRODUCTION

There's a reason I've nominated myself as your guide as you go about recording your stories: I've been on the receiving end of such a legacy.

My Story

I didn't start paying attention to my roots until after I stumbled over some of them. Now I spend a lot of my time looking for more family stories and memories.

My family tree looks nothing like the iconic oak with its rounded top and balanced, far-reaching branches. That archetype conjures images of the entire family gathered together, sharing its cooling and protective shade, drinking lemonade or other beverages while the kids climb around above. When you're trying to trace your ancestors' stories, though, the experience just doesn't seem as symmetrical or accessible as the oak's branches. *Roots* seem more applicable—hidden, fragile, tangled, and often more than just a little bit dirty.

The silhouette of my tree used to look more like a willow that lost limbs in every storm, rendered lopsided by time and nature, than the archetypal oak. I had precious little information on my father's side, owing not the least to the fact that my grandmother was an orphan. The opposite was true of my mother's side of the family—I had information on our ancestors going back to about 1500.

For the intact maternal side of our tree, my sister and I had two great sources of information. One was our amazing aunt Ann and her thirty-plus years of pre-Internet genealogical research. The other was our grandmother's *Treasure Chest of Memories*, an old spiral notebook filled with a lifetime of writings—childhood memories, stories of her children as they grew, and wisdom she had gathered along the way—my inspiration for this guide.

As she approached the end of her battle with cancer, Grandma decided to pass her *Treasure Chest of Memories* on to her children and grandchildren.

My mother, the best one at deciphering grandma's handwriting, painstakingly transcribed Grandma's scrawl and presented each of her siblings and every grandchild with a folder of typed writings—our own copy of Grandma's *Treasure Chest of Memories*.

A treasure it is! Grandma died in 1983, the year I graduated from college. I was not able to enjoy a woman-to-woman relationship with her in life, but through her memories, I connect with her again and again throughout the different phases of my life.

My sister and I came to value Grandma's memories and stories even more after our parents died in an automobile accident in 1998. In the face of our loss, our grandmother's memories of our mother allowed us a semblance of continued connection to her. Grandma's *Treasure Chest of Memories* proved to be a source of great comfort.

In 2006, my family tree morphed into something more closely resembling the quintessential oak. The aforementioned and amazing Aunt Ann found a census reference to my paternal grandmother, who by her own account had lost her mother at age six and whose father had elected not to raise her. Astonishingly, a little bit of research revealed that my father's mother was not the orphan child she purported to be but rather had eleven siblings. Soon I was able to make an Internet acquaintance of one of my father's cousins that he'd never had the privilege of knowing. I could no longer view our family tree and its missing branches as a victim of the comparatively benign forces of time and weather. Our tree now seemed like an old soldier, a survivor that had weathered the storms of wanton chainsaw-bearing human forces.

I felt a strong sense of deprivation on my father's behalf and was outraged at the family connections denied to him, an only child. My paternal grandmother's denial of her family roots did, however, bring home the incalculable value of a family Treasure Chest. Our lack of knowledge about her and our lack of connection with her past are great losses. They stand in glaring juxtaposition to the legacy left by my maternal grandmother, whose stories connect us—her children, their spouses, and all fourteen of us cousins—not only to her, but also to each other.

Why is this loss of connection so immense? Why is the preservation of connections such a gift?

Ultimately, what matters most in life are our connections to our family and loved ones. When a life ends, display boards at the viewing or wake never reflect the departed's financial status or executive accomplishments. Instead, they display photos of that person in the places they loved, doing the things that they loved, and with the people they loved. Behind each photo is a story that still has meaning to loved ones and connects them to the life that so recently ended.

These connections are the marrow of our lives, sustaining and nourishing us from within. This life-giving marrow of stories and memories should be shared and passed on so that we can fortify our connections to each other and springboard conversations in the here and now. They also allow us to continue to connect, teach, support, and console after we're gone.

My sister started yearning for connections early in life.

I admit I'm biased. I've seen the connections forged and lives touched, and I know the doability of creating a personal Treasure Chest. This guide not only provides an outline for you to construct legacy of written memories to be treasured, but it should also motivate, challenge, encourage, and cajole you as you create a treasure of incalculable value for your loved ones. It's written in honor of my grandmother Hazel Savoy Crymes, who gave me the gift of her *Treasure Chest of Memories*.

You can't always fill in the missing branches on your family tree, but you can make the branches that are there accessible to your loved ones. Through your memories, your family tree can become the beloved shade tree in the middle of the yard under which the adults sit and on which the kids climb. You can even add a tire swing and maybe little boards up the trunk to make it easier to climb.

Creating Your Own Legacy

Creating a legacy sounds hard, but you're probably already doing it. With every mention of a memory—in a letter, post, tweet, or in person—we're forming a legacy. A *Treasure Chest* is simply a mechanism for collecting, preserving, and sharing the stories of our pasts, our personalities, and our affection for our loved ones.

Writing about your memories doesn't have to be an arduous task. Today's technology makes it easier than ever to share memories, but navigating the options, choosing which memories to write about, figuring out how to format and share them, and contending with that nagging self-doubt every writer experiences can be intimidating. That's where *Memories of Me* comes in. This guide will help you figure out exactly what kind of Treasure Chest you'd like to create, what you want to put in it, how often you want to fill it, and to what extent you want to share its contents. In-depth brainstorming worksheets, writing exercises, and examples accompany each starter topic to stimulate your recall and foster your creativity. Though I discourage perfectionism, I've included just enough writing advice to make sure you're satisfied with your final product. You don't need to have award-winning writing, scrapbooking, or photography skills. You just need to have a desire to connect with your loved ones.

How to Use This Guide

If you want to get the most out of this book, you need to read and write. Obviously, I want you to read the whole book, but I hope you don't do it all at once. Put it down often. Experiment as you go. Read a section, then use the worksheets or exercises and start writing. This book is meant to be a companion and a guide—one that's more interested in seeing you enjoy your journey than it is in making sure you get every footfall right or even seeing that you stay on the path I might have chosen. It's your journey, so you get to beat your own trail. Like a good companion, this book will give encouragement from time to time, keep an eye out for dangerous pitfalls, and remind you to take in the scenic overlooks.

Printable copies of the worksheets throughout this book can be found at cedarfort.com/memories. These PDF versions, which provide space for your responses, are available for readers' personal use. You can also use a dedicated notebook so you can easily revisit your thoughts.

You'll also find examples of my writing and illustrations throughout this book. They are the results of my own journey compiling a Treasure Chest, which is my primary motivation to nominate myself as your guide. They do not purport to be the absolute model of journalistic or literary excellence (or anything close to that), but they serve to show you how doable the journey is.

Though I've started out on the path before you, I'm no Sherpa. I can't "carry" everything you need to record your memories. You don't have to be a Sherpa either, however. As you embark on your adventure of writing, try not to get frustrated. Like life itself, it's the journey, or, in this case, the process of remembering and writing, that matters more than any one destination, how long you travel, or what roads you take. Be sure you take the time to enjoy each stop, focusing on the connections you are forging with your past and your loved ones as you write. As you keep your loved ones in mind—and write about the people, places, and things you love—you will fully enjoy the process, improve your writing, and avoid the roadblocks (and writer's blocks) along the way.

Part 1

Getting Started

BRINGING YOUR MEMORIES TO LIFE

Bringing your collection of memories and stories to life involves more than confronting that ever-intimidating blank screen or page. It involves figuring out what treasures you possess and which ones you're going to pack in your Chest. How methodical you are as you embark on this adventure of establishing a legacy of memories will depend on your personality. If you're like me and have little propensity for forethought and planning, you'll want to dig right in, figuring out your mistakes and regrouping along the way.

Enthusiasm and momentum are good things, especially in writing, and I certainly don't want to slow you down if you're on a roll. On the other hand, spending a little time contemplating your motivations for preserving memories can facilitate your writing and help you make decisions as the structure of your Treasure Chest evolves. It can also prevent frustration. Consider the following:

What Do You Want to Preserve?

Paradoxically, in this case, answering the *what* can help you articulate the *why*.

Your motivation might be as simple as the urge to preserve the past for yourself and others. It's a great service to future generations, and the process of remembering brings enjoyment, regrounds us, and connects us to our past. There's honor in that alone, but there are also secondary benefits. By recording memories, you'll leave a part of yourself behind for your readers. They will view the past through the filter of your writing and, by extension, will have a glimpse into your life and a connection with you. They won't simply learn what happened to you; they'll learn to *know* you. Your stories will preserve your family history and your place in it for future generations.

There may be more to it, however, than the simple yet noble sharing of past events. If you're more creative, you may want to incorporate your artistic side into your Treasure Chest, enriching your narrations with your personal style or literary artfulness. You can also include your artwork (or scans or photos of it), scrapbook layouts, and the like. You can also accomplish this through the way you choose to package your Treasure Chest, which you can read more about in "Recording Your Stories: Choose Your Medium Well."

Consider going beyond a simple glimpse into the past. Use your writing as a vehicle to connect with others on a much more personal level. Even if you are not normally a heart-on-your-sleeve person, think carefully about leaving a legacy to a larger part of yourself—your feelings and reflections. Those who love you will appreciate not only knowing what happened in your past but knowing how you felt about it then and how you feel about it now. This openness can cement the connections of a shared past or ancestry and can spark meaningful conversations and understanding among your loved ones.

My grandmother did this in her Treasure Chest. I'm sure it was difficult for her to reveal her frailty in writing. However, because of her willingness to write about and share her moments of loss, grief, and doubt, I feel a deep bond with her. Only you, however, can decide how much of yourself you will ultimately reveal to others.

Of course, that begs another question.

Who Is It for?

You might be writing for yourself. There's nothing selfish about this. You don't have to feel compelled to share your memories to be motivated to preserve them. You might want to preserve your stories while memory serves or while health still permits you to write and enjoy them. You might write to work through your feelings about your past to reconnect yourself with your roots, process your grief at the loss of a loved one, or simply for the joy of writing.

Many of us do find that our enjoyment of remembering multiplies as memories are shared, motivating us to share our writing or even write for others. The resulting dialogues deepen our connections to those who read them. As we share, we often find that others reciprocate our sharing, enhancing our memories with memories of their own.

Chronic, debilitating, or terminal illnesses can also be catalysts for preserving memories. It's not only for themselves that these patients feel driven to document the past before it is lost to them; it's their legacy for their loved ones too. Especially for those who find that their illness prevents them from actively taking a part in the lives of family and friends, writing can affirm that they were there in spirit—cheering on kids, wiping tears, crossing fingers, and swelling with pride. Years later, through their writing, they can be there to teach, comfort, and encourage.

Sharing the past can bring understanding to fragmented families, kindle meaningful conversations, and lead to insights that otherwise might never take place. It can open lines of communications that connect loved ones to their common heritage. For this reason, family historians don't just leave names and dates on pedigree charts; they enhance their ancestry sheets with narrations of events from long ago, a great service both to far-removed family members and generations to come They don't just document where ancestors came from, they document who those ancestors were.

The ultimate motivation for sharing is the feeling that you get when you realize your writing has moved or brought joy to someone else. There's nothing quite like that. However, when it comes to motivation, there often isn't just *one* answer, much less a *right* answer. We're motivated by a combination of factors, and our answers may change from time to time as well. My answer might not be yours.

Excogitating (mentally chewing on) these points will help you assemble your Treasure Chest. They will help you know your audience and thus facilitate your writing, and they can also help you make decisions as the final shape and format of your Treasure Chest emerges. Though you may not be sure of the answers, contemplating what they might be will help you determine how much of your more vulnerable side you are willing to share as you put your memories to paper.

Once you have a broad idea of how you would like to go forward, do it. Your decisions are not final at this point, and you can always fine-tune or readjust later. Don't allow planning to curb your creativity.

RECORDING YOUR STORIES: CHOOSE YOUR MEDIUM WELL

Deciding what your Treasure Chest will look like entails making decisions about the format and medium you're going to use to write, preserve, and present your memories. Once again, there is no right answer or perfect formula, and your decisions are not engraved in stone. To do it well, you simply have to do what is right for you and what works for you.

There are at least three good options. As you go through them and weigh the pros and cons of each, also give thought to which will fit best into your lifestyle and which is the best match for your personality and proclivities. Just because something is a good idea doesn't necessarily mean that it is a good idea for *you*.

Handwritten Journal

If you love the feel of pen and paper, there is no need to go high tech. Find a notebook or attractive journal and just get started. Handwritten words are becoming more and more of a treasure. In fact, the handwriting of a loved one can evoke strong emotions and facilitate connections. Perhaps that's why so many of us prefer receiving a handwritten letter or card over an email. If you write legibly, your family will almost certainly enjoy and even treasure seeing your hand.

This is a lesson my family learned the hard way. My grandmother's handwriting was illegible. In fact, her handwriting—the term *handwriting* itself is perhaps generous—was self-taught and looked more like a toddler's imitation of cursive. If not for my mother's ability to decipher it and her determination to record my grandmother's writings for the rest of us, Grandma's whole Treasure Chest might have been lost to us. Though my mother typed Grandma's memories, she annotated many in her own hand.

Somehow, my mother's handwriting embodies her personality. When I look at it, my heart inevitably experiences a tug.

Author Chris Gayomali makes some convincing arguments that "handwriting may be a lost art, but it's still an invaluable skill."[1] Not only do some famous and not-so-famous writers love the slowness and intentionality of handwriting, some experts argue that it increases focus and recall.[2]

Digital (Computer) Archiving

Your comfort level with computer and Internet technology will have a strong correlation with your choice to go digital or not. For many, the decision is a no-brainer, but if you're not sure, ask yourself some basic questions: Do you find word-processing programs to be your most efficient way of putting words to paper? Do you like the convenience of editing, sorting, cutting, and pasting? Do you find paperless files easier to organize? Do you have a readily available (and working) laptop, tablet, or desktop computer? (This one can be a deal breaker.)

If your answers were more along the lines of "Perish the thought!" or if the questions themselves filled you with distaste, don't feel like you have to force yourself to use media with which you are uncomfortable. These are simply options. Whether you experiment or not is up to you. You'll write best when you're comfortable with your tools.

If you answered "Yes" the above questions—or even most of them— digital media is probably for you. You can write at will, edit later, and insert and resize images. Working on your PC, tablet, or laptop does not preclude leaving behind an actual ink-on-paper book for others. There are many reasonably priced programs and websites for self-publishing your project.

Not a good typist? Particularly if you finger-peck or find typing laborious, voice-recognition technology is worth considering. This technology has made great advances in recent years, making the dictation of stories a realistic option. A variety of software packages on the market allow your speech to generate text in your word-processing program, which then provides you with the same ease of editing and formatting your final product.

There's another advantage to using your PC, laptop, or tablet: if you later decide to put your memories on a blog, you can simply cut and paste your entries into the blogging program of your choice.

Important Note about Digital Storage: To protect yourself against loss from accidental deletion or hard drive crashes, you should *absolutely* make yourself backup copies as you work. You can use CDs, an external hard drive, or an Internet-based storage system like Dropbox or Google Drive.

Blogging

If you're computer and Internet savvy and would like to share your memories in real time, a blog might be the best option. Because a Treasure Chest is episodic in nature, it lends itself easily to blogging. Blogs offer the capability of inserting not only images but audio and video files as well, enabling you to include old film clips or recorded interviews with relatives. Blog platforms also allow increased organizational flexibility with their tagging systems. Unlike traditional file folders (manila or digital), these do not require you to choose a single keyword under which you'll store an entry. A single post can have numerous tags at once, such as memories, children, family, faith, and humor, enabling you to categorize a narrative in a number of ways and help readers navigate their way through your writings.

Many free and easy-to-use blog programs are available over the Internet with preset appearance and layout themes (see Recommended Resources for more information). You have the option to make your blog private so that only your family (or whomever else you have issued a password to) has access, or you can share posts with the world at large (or at least the part of the world that reads blogs). Family members can comment on your memories as you go and augment them with their own memories, versions, or their own blog entries. In turn, you and other blog readers can respond to their comments, which can result in some lively conversations. Readers can also subscribe to receive email notifications of new posts. However, you don't have to share anything until you're ready. You can store your posts as drafts until you are ready to reveal them to others.

You don't have to make a decision at the outset on whether you're going to store your writings on your own computer or create and store them online. You can always upload your word processor files to your favorite blog site when you've finished editing. This way, you have a copy of all your Treasure Chest entries on your own hard drive, where you can enjoy the ease of formatting and spellchecking in your office program. You can consider blogging as your project progresses and make your decision later.

As in the previous section, there is no right or wrong answer here. As you work, you can adapt and change, but it *does* help to consider your options as you begin. You simply have to find what is most comfortable for you.

1. Chris Gayomali, "4 benefits of writing by hand," The Week Publications, Inc. (January 16, 2013), http://theweek.com/article/index/238801/4-benefits-of-writing-by-hand.
2. Ibid.

FINDING TIME TO WRITE

The very doggedness of time's forward march that inspires writers to preserve memories in the first place is often the largest obstacle they encounter as they start writing. Time seems especially elusive when it comes to those projects that are floating around in our brains as mere good intentions. The good news is that we can all carve out time to write. As a longtime and accomplished procrastinator, I can attest to this.

So how do you stop procrastinating? How do you make time to write? As this doesn't come naturally to me, I had to do some research. Reviewing what various authors wrote about transforming writing from procrastination to a passion, I came upon almost unanimous advice: make writing a habit.

It's that simple. It's that hard.

Wanting to write and intending to write are not enough. Writing, like playing an instrument, gets easier and sounds better the more you practice. Likewise, the more you find time to practice, the more enjoyable it will be to play. Good habits rarely spring to life on their own; they are the results of discipline and desire. The desire part can come fairly easily. The discipline might need a game plan. Several points seem standard across writing advice sources. Not surprisingly, they are the ones that I personally found most helpful.

Make Writing a Priority

Consciously or unconsciously, we prioritize our daily tasks. We have things that absolutely have to be done, things that we mean to do, and things that would be nice to get done. Even among the things that we absolutely have to do, we prioritize. To keep writing on your radar, you need to decide how often you want to write and create a realistic schedule for writing. If it's not to fall in between the cracks, that schedule has to be a priority.

Luckily, once you've established a routine, it becomes much easier to stick to it. You don't have to categorize your writing as a world-will-end-if-I-don't-do-this priority, but it should be pretty high on the list. Some people find it helpful to enter it on their calendar or calendar app, giving it an increased aura of legitimacy.

Pick a Time to Write

Choose when to write based on your personal biorhythms, work habits, preferences, and life situation. Ideally, it should be a time of day when you are the most creative or productive as well as a time that you can realistically work. If there is a part of your day that kids, work, neighbors, or other things tend to intrude on, take the likelihood of that interruption into account when you set your goals. Don't delude yourself about your temperament and proclivities either. If you're not a morning person, don't deceive yourself into thinking that you'll get up early to write. Likewise, if late afternoon is the time of day that most of the fires flare up, plan to write in the morning.

Turn Off Distractions

If the phone, television, email, or radio distracts you, turn it off. I'm not quite clear on how to turn off kids, but that might also be worth a try. If you work best in quiet, find a relatively quiet place and time to work. If you're not sure what time will work best for you, experiment with some different times of the day.

What is a distraction to one person might be just the thing to get the next person in their groove. Not everyone, for instance, works best in complete silence. If noise, particularly white noise, isn't a distraction for you, there's no need to turn it off. For most of us, it's really a matter of finding the right level of noise. Many people focus better with music in the background. Some writers do well in coffee shops while others work in quiet seclusion.[1] Once you find the conditions that work best for you, write under those conditions whenever you can.

Set Realistic Goals

Make *realistic* a mantra. Don't set yourself up for failure by setting unreasonable goals. No one wants to keep working on a task at which he or she repeatedly fails. If you are currently working multiple jobs or working full-time and raising children, it may not be realistic to expect yourself to write one hour a day. Set a goal that you can achieve with a little discipline.

Perhaps you can only carve out time a couple of times a week. If you need to challenge yourself as your Treasure Chest develops, you can adjust your goals. Setting realistic goals will assure that you are able to enjoy success, which brings us to the topic of keeping yourself motivated.

Reward Yourself

Go ahead and do more than bask in the intrinsic value of a job well done. Experts recommend that you reward yourself in a tangible way. It might be sharing your writing with a friend, getting an ice-cream cone, taking a walk, or—my personal favorite—eating chocolate. The important thing is to acknowledge and celebrate your progress. Defining your rewards in advance will give you a reason to work for them, or at least an incentive to stay focused. This goes hand in hand with setting realistic goals, so be sure you set reasonable thresholds before you give yourself a pat on the back.

Don't Expect Unwavering Inspiration

We start out gung-ho and full of ideas, but soon we are plowed flat by those other good intentions that are haphazardly paving our roads. So many writers' advice columns address this that I can only assume that many would-be memoirists crash after the light of their initial inspiration burns dim. The advice gurus admonish us to keep writing and preserve our stories. Inspiration, like ideas, comes in fits and starts. There will inevitably be days when we have a lot of fits but few starts. There might even be days when we're tempted to throw fits. When inspiration fails, we have to keep on working. (This might well be where the discipline kicks in.)

This advice is meant for professional writers, but just think how much more relevant it is for those of us that have the luxury of writing for people who love us rather than for a Pulitzer Prize. Not everything has to be spectacularly funny or poignant. Sometimes, our stories are just stories. The less-inspired memory will clean up nicely with a little editing.

I am reminded of one of my teenage son's soccer teammates begging, "Coach! Take me out. I suck today!" The coach refused, saying, "Son, you've got to learn to play through it. Keep playing!" So when the words don't seem to flow as well as you're used to them flowing, play (or write) through it.

Keep a Notepad Handy

The brain is a quirky organ and will decide to spit out ideas at the oddest times. Sometimes our creativity outpaces our memory. My creativity definitely outpaces my organization. As a result, I have various piles of scrap paper, paper bags, church bulletins, brochures, and Post-It Notes with scribbled ideas. Avoid emulating me—when a good idea surfaces, don't count on being able to recall it later. Keep a notepad and pencil handy and scratch yourself a reminder, or keep a page in your smartphone, tablet, or PDA for that purpose. (There will be more about this in the "Keeping Track of Ideas" section.)

As you find the time to write, you'll also find the time to grow and, sometimes, even heal. Embrace that. Writing about your memories requires processing them to some degree, and that process of reflection can bring enjoyment and peace. An inherent satisfaction comes with putting memories on paper. That satisfaction is multiplied when others gain enjoyment or enlightenment by reading what you've written.

1. Sikstrom, Sverker, Andrew Smart, and Goran Soderlund. "Listen to the noise: noise is beneficial for cognitive performance in ADHD." Journal of Child Psychology and Psychiatry 48.8 (2007): 840-847. Academic OneFile. Web. 11 Mar. 2014, .http://dbproxy.fh.farmlib.org:2305/ps/i.do?id=GALE%7CA284141732&v=2.1&u =lom_metronetmnfc&it=r&p=AONE&sw=w&asid=faf4cac5cce3dcb002679cecc8 dc805d.

BRAINSTORM-A-COMING

Stories come to life from ideas and memories. The first step to writing is getting your ideas and memories out of your brain and onto paper. This is sometimes more easily said than done, typed, or written. You just want to get your thoughts rolling, unimpeded by editing, trimming, or politeness.

The analogy of a storm is apt. Your ideas, once they start, should not drizzle down slowly and neatly, but should come in a barrage or in intermittent bursts. In addition, like the weather, your brainstorm results will vary from day to day. Some days the barometer will be rising, and you'll have a wealth of ideas. Other days, the storm will quickly be over, or the precipitation will be limited to a drizzle. For this reason, you shouldn't consider your brainstorming sheets as single-use tools. Whether you use the ones provided here or make your own, keep your brainstorming sheets dynamic. Come back to them from time to time and add new ideas. As you do, you'll be able to watch your framework of ideas grow and mature.

It is important to note that brainstorm sheets are a springboard or starting gate, *not* a final product. You might reject many of the things you write down, or you may find some subjects too difficult to master (or even to contemplate)—especially at the beginning. That's okay; this is not a stage for perfectionism. It's a way to get started.

To begin, find a quiet place and a small block of time. Start brainstorming. In many sections of this book, brainstorming sheets are included for your convenience, but these are not your only options. You can write in any type of word processing document, portable device like a tablet or smartphone, or use any type of paper and pen or pencil. Use whatever sparks your creativity. There are, however, a few rules. Even if you have perfectionist proclivities, bear with them. Brainstorming exercises are designed to maximize creativity and minimize inertia.

The Rules of the Storm:

- Do not use full sentences.
- Do not edit.
- Correct spelling is optional.
- Neatness does not count.
- Wait and review later.

As you can see, there is just one point of these exercises: getting your ideas from your brain onto your paper. When your storm peters out a bit, give yourself a break. Creativity is erratic and capricious. The "wait and review later" process works much better than trying to force ideas out of a brain that is no longer in the mood to cooperate.

The brainstorming worksheets included throughout this book are meant to assist you. They're a great way to start. Use them when you find them helpful, but feel free to adapt them or use your own. Try starting with the exercises that follow and see how they work for you. These focus on figuring out whom you want to write about and which people have most influenced you. Later you will narrow that focus. Whatever format you use, remember to save your ideas for future reference so that you can come back to them a little later and add new ideas. Over time, they will become a source of writing inspiration.

Additional Tools:

Brainstorming Exercise provides warm-up exercises to get you thinking about your memories and practice brainstorming.

Printable copies of the worksheets throughout this book can be found at cedarfort.com/memories. These PDF versions, which provide space for your responses, are available for readers' personal use. You can also use a dedicated notebook so you can easily revisit your thoughts.

Worksheet: Brainstorming Exercise

Warm up:

Get your pen or pencil ready. In twenty seconds, write down every word that comes into your mind when you hear the word tree. Remember the rules: no full sentences, no editing, correct spelling is completely optional, neatness does not count, and wait and review later.

Who:

Give yourself a couple of minutes on this one: Who are the most important people in your life?

Who II:

Again, give yourself a couple of minutes: Looking back on your life, who were the people that influenced you most?

Now that you've practiced brainstorming, look at your results. Try writing about a memory of someone you've brainstormed.

OUTLINING—TO BE
OR NOT TO BE

Before you decide if you need to develop an outline for your project, first consider whether your project needs to have a certain shape or if you have a deadline. Implicit in that consideration is a decision about the length and scope of your project. For instance, if you are getting your Treasure Chest ready for a family reunion a few months away, an outline could help narrow your scope to stories related to that side of your family, stories most in danger of being forgotten, or simply the number of stories that you can realistically get done in that time. With a due date in mind, using an outline will help ensure that the most important points for your loved ones are covered.

Without a due date, or when you've already focused your topics somewhat, the need for an outline might not be as critical. My grandmother left us a perfectly beautiful Treasure Chest without using a framework at all. Her writing was her hobby and her therapy, and those who received her legacy were secondary beneficiaries. She wrote what she was moved to write when she was moved to write it. She probably never had a firm idea of who she wanted to share it with or how. Part of the charm of her Treasure Chest is its free-form nature.

Of course, there is a middle ground. If you don't have time constraints for your project, you might want to leave it more open ended, allowing your project to shape itself somewhat. Your stories will fall into some type of topical order. William Zinsser, indisputable master on the craft of writing and author of *On Writing Well*, suggests simply writing every day for several months, then printing out all your pieces and laying them out in front of you. As you re-read your writing, patterns and themes in your writing will become apparent.[1] Similarly, taking your brainstorming notes and reordering them and annotating them to some degree can reveal a natural, workable framework.

Outlines or similar frameworks are not just helpful for organizing a Treasure Chest; they can also help with two quandaries we might face. Some of us aren't sure we will have enough memorable material for a legacy while others look upon the richness of their past and can't possibly imagine where they'd start or end. For the former, an outline can act as a guide and memory prompter, helping to bring the most vivid moments to mind. If the latter dilemma is your problem, an outline can also help limit the scope of your writing and thus make the undertaking less overwhelming. You can use it along with your *Who is it for?* and *What do I want to preserve?* considerations to narrow your choices and focus your writing.

The final and perhaps most important determining factor is going to be your personality and your love or lack of tolerance for order. Some people thrive in more structured environments and find that having a framework in place allows their thoughts to flow better. Others find more comfort in a bare-bones outline or framework, feeling more creative with fewer constraints. Again, there is no right or wrong way to proceed. You will write best when you choose the type of guide that best suits you.

1. William Zinsser, *On Writing Well: The Classic Guide to Writing Non-Fiction*, 30th Anniversary ed. (New York: Harper-Collins, 2006), 293–94.

KEEP YOUR DATES

Many stories and narratives are timeless, but that doesn't mean that they won't benefit from the addition of a date or two. As a genealogy buff, I have a special love for dates. Not only do dates eliminate the blank spots on cascading pedigree charts, they also lend historical perspective. Awareness of the time periods in which our ancestors lived can fill in details between the bare facts provided by comparatively bland church, military, and government records.

Genealogists are not the only ones that benefit from the inclusion of dates, however. Writers of both fiction and nonfiction use historical perspectives to give their readers insight into characters' lives, allowing readers to infer or fill in details based on the circumstances of time and place.

Time can be as important as place in providing a setting. For instance, my husband's grandfather was a linesman for the telephone company. Without any historical context, you'd imagine him to be like linesmen you see working today. However, with the additional information that he was a linesman in the 1920s, your imagination takes a different turn. You might see him more as he perhaps saw himself—as a trailblazer making the way for the inevitable progress of technology. Including even a brief amount of historical context not only helps orient your reader, but it also lends a deeper understanding of why events may have happened as they did.

This doesn't mean you have to know or research the exact date. Keep in mind that a historical reference point is not simply a date or a decade. It can be any reference that orients your readers to the environment in which your narrative occurred. It could be during wartime, the Depression, civil rights demonstrations, or a certain phase of life, such as "when the kids were still in diapers" or "before cars were equipped with turn indicators." Such added detail not only gives your memories more texture, it helps ensure that your readers will fully understand the story you're telling.

In fact, such time references can be helpful when you'd like to call attention to how your memory is particularly ironic or impressive when juxtaposed against its historical backdrop. For example, if readers are on their toes, they'll realize the significance of a biracial marriage in 1968. However, if you state that a biracial marriage took place in the same year and state as the assassination of Martin Luther King Jr., your readers cannot overlook the significance.

As you write about your memories, try to illuminate your narratives with time references and historical perspectives. Use relevant vocabulary, such as *cable cars*, *speakeasy*, and *groovy*. I've included a worksheet to help you establish timelines for your stories. Even if your recall is not precise, the more information your readers have, the greater the ease with which their imaginations can accompany you on your walks down memory lane.

Additional Tools:

Worksheet: Establishing a Timeline of Events helps you establish time references for your memories.

Sample Worksheet: Establishing a Timeline of Events provides an illustration of a completed timeline exercise.

My Turn: Half-Full illustrates how time references can enhance a narrative.

Establishing a Timeline of Events

This simple tool should help you establish an overview of the events of your life. On the left side of the time line, fill in the increments as they relate to the year of your birth. On the right side of the time line, jot down events (moves, marriages, divorces, births, relationships, graduations, jobs, career changes, trips, and other turning points) that happened during that time period. On the far right, add events that might provide historical context.

	Events	**Historical Context**

Your birth year : _____

Your birth year + 10: _____

Your birth year + 20: _____

Your birth year + 30: _____

Your birth year + 40: _____

Your birth year + 50: _____

Your birth year + 60: _____

Your birth year + 70: _____

Your birth year + 80: _____

Your birth year + 90: _____

Sample Worksheet: Timeline of Events

This is how a personal timeline might turn out:

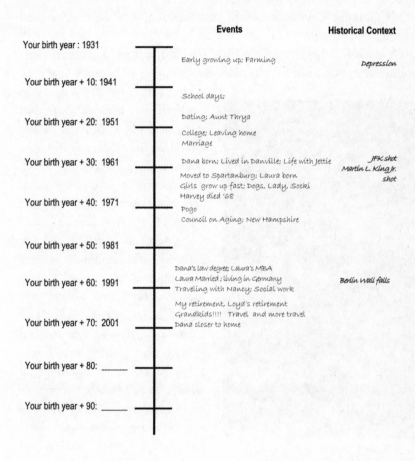

Events   **Historical Context**

Your birth year : 1931

Early growing up; Farming   Depression

Your birth year + 10: 1941

School days;

Your birth year + 20: 1951

Dating; Aunt Thrya

College; Leaving home
Marriage

Your birth year + 30: 1961

Dana born; Lived in Danville; Life with Jettie   JFK shot
Martin L. Kling Jr.
Moved to Spartanburg; Laura born   shot
Girls grow up fast; Dogs, Lady, Socki
Harvey died '68

Your birth year + 40: 1971

Pogo
Council on Aging; New Hampshire

Your birth year + 50: 1981

Dana's law degree; Laura's MBA
Laura Married ; living in Germany   Berlin Wall falls

Your birth year + 60: 1991

Traveling with Nancy; Social work

My retirement, Loyd's retirement
Grandkids!!!! Travel and more travel

Your birth year + 70: 2001

Dana closer to home

Your birth year + 80: _____

Your birth year + 90: _____

My Turn: Half-Full

Note: As you read the story, pay close attention to the italicized sentences. How do they help you more fully understand the subject portrayed?

Is the cup half-empty or half-full?

My Grandpa Crymes answered that question with the way he lived his faith.

Grandpa had health problems in his youth that left him frail, causing him to walk with difficulty. *My mom always tried to sell it as a good thing, pointing out that it kept him home from two world wars,* but even as a child, I always looked at Grandpa's life situation with more than a little pity. His limp, which became more crippling with age, made working his Virginia tobacco farm physically difficult.

Durrell Crymes, my grandpa

Mom always described her parents' socioeconomic status growing up as "dirt poor." *During the '30s they didn't always have enough to eat or to feed their four children. They also lost a child during that time. They finally upgraded to indoor plumbing at some point in the '60s, but even in the relative prosperity of the '70s and '80s they didn't have much.* In grandpa's book, having less than others was no reason to be ungrateful. Up until he had a stroke in his eighties, every night, my grandpa would literally get down on his knees by his bed to say his prayers. In his later years, it might take him five or ten minutes to get down on his knees from his walker or wheelchair, but he did it. He didn't do it to ask God for things. Although it might not have looked that way to others, and although I might not have been convinced of the fact, Grandpa knew he was blessed. He did it to thank the Lord for what he had.

Because of this lesson of faith that my grandfather taught me, I finally grew to understand that Grandpa was indeed blessed. Now, when I dream my dreams for my own life, I dream of having the same blessings that Grandpa and Grandma had. I dream of a home with jokes and laughter. I dream of children that still love each other and their parents deeply, long into their adult lives. I dream of those children having the education that will enable them to pursue careers of their choice successfully. I dream of friendships that are unshakable, unmarred by time and circumstance. I dream of having an unshakable faith. I dream of treasuring my moments.

Because Grandpa's glass was way more than half-full, I try to teach my children the importance of that same dream. I also dream that regardless of how life looks to the rest of us, their glasses will always be filled to the brim.

VISUAL AIDS

Creativity should be your guide in assembling your Treasure Chest, but as a communicator, you want to maximize your readers' experience by making it easier for them to absorb and understand your writing. Luckily, by simply keeping a few key precepts about the reader in mind, it isn't difficult to balance your personal self-expression with the readability and digestibility of your Treasure Chest.

Choose a Readable Font

The font (typeface) you choose will affect your readers' ability to digest your stories and reflections. Choose a font that is easy to read, or, if you are handwriting your Treasure Chest, make sure your writing is legible. This does not simply mean selecting a twelve-point font. The typeface you use should not have so many curlicues or other decorations that a reader has to decipher instead of read. Save those fonts for the titles—if you use them at all.

This may seem nitpicky at first, but experts regard it as critically important. Font recommendations are based on quite a bit of research.[1] If your choice of format is a blog or other online media, these considerations become even more important and more complex. Most typographers have different font choices for printed matter versus blogs or websites. (See Recommended Resources for more information.)

This isn't to say that you have no choices. Design specialists have put heart and soul in adding feeling and personality to these "standard" fonts. Visual arts journalist Rick Poynor asserts, "Type is saying things to us all the time. Typefaces express a mood, an atmosphere. They give words a certain coloring."[2] What a typeface says varies greatly with personal interpretation. For instance, many consider Helvetica to be one of the preeminent professional typefaces, but my son refers to it as "a boring typeface made by some Swedish dudes." Once you've eliminated the ones that won't work for your readers, the final decision about a font often boils down to personal appeal. Chances are the font that appeals to you the most will also best express your personality. (If you can't decide, Rick Poynor also has a "What Font Are You" test available on the web,[3] but I must confess a degree of disappointment in being identified as Times New Roman.)

In addition to font complexity considerations, bloggers need to keep font and background color considerations in mind as well. If you use anything other than black fonts on a white background, you'll have to make sure your color choices do not make your text unappealing or difficult to read

Read the following anecdote, "Come in Mr. Wind," with varying fonts. First, we'll start with a basic font in black on a white background:

> My grandmother was always cheerful, even in the face of the unexpected. But one day, she left her own self speechless.
>
> When she heard the screen door on the front of the house open, knowing that none of her family members were going in or out, she cheerfully called, "Come in, Mr. Wind!"
>
> To her great unnerving, in walked the pastor, Reverend Wind.

Next, the same text in an elaborate font demonstrates how the font's complexity can obscure the meaning of text when the reader cannot quickly make out the words:

> **𝔐𝔶 grandmother was always cheerful, even in the face of the unexpected. But one day, she left her own self speechless.**
>
> **When she heard the screen door on the front of the house open, knowing that none of her family members were going in or out, she cheerfully called, "Come in, Mr. Wind!"**
>
> **To her great unnerving, in walked the pastor, Reverend Wind.**

Even though the font is large, the now-familiar text takes a minute to decode. In a longer paragraph, reading would quickly become arduous. For this reason, many experts recommend using fancy fonts only for groups of six words or less. Employ interesting typefaces for titles and emphasis, but stick with the easily readable fonts for longer passages.

Similarly, some color combinations of background and font colors can also make your text more difficult to read. The use of opposite colors, such as green text on a red background, can fatigue the eyes.[4] Although complementary colors are indeed eye-catching, the colors do nothing to draw readers into the text. Some readers may even find it too hard to work through the story. Think carefully about who your readers are likely to be and how they'll respond to the colors you choose.

Even the standard white-on-black combination can create too much contrast for older eyes. However, there's a simple fix for this. As the below sample illustrates, changing the black to a dark gray maintains enough contrast to make text easy to discern, but eliminates glare:

> My grandmother was always cheerful, even in the face of the unexpected. But one day, she left her own self speechless.
>
> When she heard the screen door on the front of the house open, knowing that none of her family members were going in or out, she cheerfully called, "Come in, Mr. Wind!"
>
> To her great unnerving, in walked the pastor, Reverend Wind.

This is not to say that your Treasure Chest should be boring or that there is no room for creativity. For example, if you want to use certain colors but find that they are not optically appealing, you don't automatically have to scratch your preferences. By adjusting the saturation and brightness of colors, you can achieve easy compromises. Just as you can adjust a black background to gray to reduce eyestrain, reducing the saturation of background colors eliminates the optical jiggle effect created by some color combinations. You can also reserve your boldest colors for outlines and borders. (See Recommended Resources for more information.)

Another trick that many publications use to make the printing more appealing on the page is to use plenty of white space. *White space* just means that you leave ample space between lines, use standard margins, and avoid cramming information onto a page. Instead of single-spacing your text, increase your line space to 1.15 or 1.25 to ease the burden on your readers' eyes. (If you're not sure how to do this in your word processing software, click on "help" or the question mark icon and type in "line spacing.") You can also decrease the intimidation factor of a long text by using subheadings. They not only increase white space but also draw your readers into the text by telling them what's to come.

You definitely want to let your personality to come through your writing, and that may include the aesthetic aspects of your words on the page or screen. The challenge comes in balancing your personal style with your readers' needs. You certainly don't want to create optical barriers that prevent your readers from becoming invested in your writing.

Using Photos or Illustrations

Traditionally, illustrations have been much more popular in journals than photographs. If you have the artistic ability, by all means illustrate your memories. Hand illustrations will be deeply cherished by your posterity and will lend your collection a level of creativity and a unique character that photographs alone cannot achieve. If you are using a digital medium and already have artwork that you would like to incorporate, you can scan your artwork and insert the scanned images into your document. You can even resize and adjust your images as you go. Either way, your artistic work will enhance your writings and will be another treasure in your chest.

Technology has made it simple, even fun, for us to illustrate our texts. It is now much simpler to get digital copies of our photos, quickly print them or insert via our software, and add them to our journals—especially if we have chosen to write and edit on a computer, laptop, or tablet.

Captions

Using creative captions with your photographs or illustrations can also enhance your writing. If you're scanning photos out of an old photo album, consider preserving the original caption in some way. To preserve it digitally, you can scan the album pages with the original caption, use the caption as part of the scanned file's name, or use the captioning function of your photo-organizing software. That way, when you use that image in your writing, you'll have access to the caption the original owner of the photo album used. Likewise, as you're scanning, don't forget to keep track of any inscriptions you find on the back of the photo. These often work quite well as captions.

There will inevitably be times that you find a picture that you'd like to use but about which you have no details or background. In these cases, allow yourself some creative license. For instance, I found a photo of my mother as a young woman petting a mule, but I didn't know what year it was taken in or whose mule is in it. As I was scanning the photo for a project for my sister, I reflected on the fact that my sister always lamented inheriting our father's big ears. (He was always easy to identify in any group shot.) I captioned that image as "Early on in life, Ellen shows her penchant for big-eared guys." My sister appreciated the captioned humor.

Using Historical Documents

Scanned or downloaded images of historical documents can also make great additions to your memories. Not only does this type of image provide historical context and testify to the factual correctness of your memory, the image itself helps the reader's imagination go back in time. Such documents include census images, awards, newspaper clippings, professional certifications, and birth, marriage, or death certificates. All of these are well worth seeking out.

Benefits of Visual Aids

Illustrations and images enhance the readability of your entries. A page of text with an illustration is simply more visually appealing and more likely to capture and hold your readers' attention. If you're describing a childhood home, a picture of the home will help your reader create visual images of the experiences you describe. The best illustrations are those images that not only illustrate the story but are a part of the story themselves. You, as writer and memory holder, will also more deeply value and appreciate those entries illustrated with images that portray scenes of your recollection.

You do not have to include a reference to the photograph or illustration in your narrative; a simple caption usually works quite nicely. Likewise, don't feel like you have to find a photo for everything you write about, but if you are writing a lot about an area, house, school, or neighborhood, it would be good to include a visual aid for those readers that have never been there in person. Providing a photo of a person that you remember helps your reader more fully relate to your stories. It's even better if you are in the photo with that person.

Try looking at the two examples I have included at the end of this section. They are from my journal of a trip to Africa. Their texts are identical. The first is simply a text with no images; the second is the same text illustrated with images. Which one do you find more visually appealing? Which one makes you more interested in exploring the text? I can certainly tell you which is more meaningful to me—it's the one with the photos I remember taking of the animals I saw.

Additional Tools:

My Turn: A Day in Africa and *My Turn: A Day in Africa (Illustrated)*

1. Douglas Bonneville, "How to Choose a Typeface," Smashing Magazine, March 24, 2011, http://www.smashingmagazine.com/2011/03/24/how-to-choose-a-typeface/.

2. "Memorable Quotes for Helvetica (2007)," IMDb.com, Inc., accessed November 21, 2012, http://www.imdb.com/title/tt0847817/quotes.

3. "What Font are You?" ITVS, accessed November 20, 2012, http://www.pbs.org/independentlens/helvetica/quiz.html.

4. Kasper Aaberg, "Color Contrast—all about the difference," Love of Graphics, accessed March 16, 2014, http://www.loveofgraphics.com/graphicdesign/color/colorcontrast/.

My Turn: A Day in Africa

During the process of scanning old slides, I dug out my old travel journal. The following is simply what I wrote, hoping to never forget a moment. The good news is that I haven't forgotten much.

Date: 18 Dec 1991

Place: Lake Naivasha to Masai Mara

As we drove into the park, it was almost 2 p.m.—late for lunch—but we couldn't hurry because we kept seeing animals. We found an entire pride of lions, elephants, giraffes, plus lots of antelopes that the new people—Charlotte and Richard—hadn't seen yet.

Matt and I rested until 4 p.m.—time for the afternoon drive. We [those in our mini-bus] saw a couple of other mini-buses and went to check it out. We found three cheetahs, a mom and her two young, eating their kill, a zebra. There wasn't much left of the zebra, just two hooves and a head, and a pile of intestines to one side. (Mom was working on that.) With the binoculars, we could really see the black lines on their faces. They had blood on their faces, too. Despite the blood, they were strikingly beautiful animals! David said that they'd probably been feeding for one to two hours to reduce the kill to that.

Later, we saw some buffalo. One looked like he'd seen many battles. We saw a herd of Topi with a lot of young—one still had its umbilical cord. You could see it when he stood up, which was apparently quite an effort on little spindly legs. We also saw a beautiful bird—a violet-throated roller. Not long after that, a nearby vehicle started feeding a group of baboons. David honked his horn to tell them not to do that, but to no avail. In no time flat, the baboons were on top of our vehicle trying to get in.

It started to rain. Matt and I didn't have our jackets, but none of us wanted to close the roof . . . but it eventually got too cold, so we did close it. Once we got back to the lodge, the rain started hard, even with thunder and lightning. The night before, a lion had shown up on the premises, but not tonight.

My Turn: A Day in Africa (Illustrated)

Date: 18 Dec 1991

Place: Lake Naivasha to Maria Mara

As we drove into the park, it was almost 2 p.m.—late for lunch—but we couldn't hurry because we kept seeing animals. We found an entire pride of lions, elephants, giraffes, plus lots of antelopes that the new people—Charlotte and Richard—hadn't seen yet.

Matt and I rested until 4 p.m.—time for the afternoon drive. We [those in our mini-bus] saw a couple of other mini-buses and went to check it out. We found three cheetahs, a mom and her two young, eating their kill, a zebra. There wasn't much left of the zebra, just two hooves and a head, and a pile of intestines to one side. (Mom was working on that.) With the binoculars, we could really see the black lines on their faces. They had blood on their faces, too. Despite the blood, they were strikingly beautiful animals! David said that they'd probably been feeding for one to two hours to reduce the kill to that.

Beautiful Animals!

Later, we saw some buffalo. One looked like he'd seen many battles. We saw a herd of Topi with a lot of young—one still had its umbilical cord. You could see it when he stood up, which was apparently quite an effort on little spindly legs. We also saw a beautiful bird—a violet-throated roller. Not long after that, a nearby vehicle started feeding a group of baboons. David honked his horn to tell them not to do that, but to no avail. In no time flat, the baboons were on top of our vehicle trying to get in.

It started to rain. Matt and I didn't have our jackets, but none of us wanted to close the roof . . . but it eventually got too cold, so we did close it. Once we got back to the lodge, the rain started hard, even with thunder and lightning. The night before, a lion had shown up on the premises, but not tonight.

TICKLING YOUR MEMORY

For the more distractible among us, visual cues, commonly known as household items, can cause us to go on mornings-long journeys of distractions. We go through the master bedroom with the intent of cleaning the bathtub, but on the way spot an item out of place. Taking that item towards the laundry room, we realize we might as well do a load of wash while we're at it. Noticing that we're low on detergent, we go into the kitchen to make a note of it. In the kitchen, we see the dog that needs walking. While walking the dog . . . and so on.

While that kind of distraction can be catastrophic for the bathtub yearning to be cleaned, visual cues can facilitate highly productive brainstorming. They tickle our memory and take us back to places and events we haven't thought about in years.

Find the visual cues that titillate your memory. Start with old photos or filmstrips and let yourself be sidetracked. This will assist you in your brainstorming, and looking back on the images of people in your past can also be enjoyable. Other great resources are memorabilia such as marked-up maps, postcards, and souvenirs from travels and vacations, as well as cards and letters from friends and relatives that you may have saved. Have you inherited boxes of papers and clippings? Go through them. Let your mind wander, but keep a pencil and paper with you as you try to keep up!

TRUTH AND ACCURACY

The truth of the matter is that memory is often imperfect. This ethereal nature of memory can leave memory collectors struggling to maintain truth and accuracy in their stories. As you gather and write your stories, you may find yourself wearing a couple of different hats. The role you're playing as you write a particular story will determine whether your writing reflects truth, accuracy, or both.

Wearing the Family Historian Hat

If you're compiling narratives to augment or replace family tree information, accuracy will matter. You'll want to interject phrases such as "according to [Source]" and "though no sources could be found." That's because a historian is not only charged with researching but also with certifying facts with a variety of sources. This isn't to say that the family historian can't write about stories based on lore. First, you can cite the source—your family member that did the original telling. Second, stories for which no sources are known can be told as just that—unsourced stories. Even if genealogy isn't your thing, if you do have some facts, you can do the future family historian a favor by including them. Birthdates, places of birth, addresses, and maiden names can be immensely helpful to those researching family lines. If family history is your focus, don't forget, your biggest gift to your ancestors is the fact that you'll be bringing them to life via your stories and memories.

Wearing the Storyteller's Hat

Storytelling and writing aren't the same craft. There are people who have wonderful writing mechanics and style but can't spin a good yarn. Others may not be excellent writers but can tell compelling stories. Photojournalists, for example, are often great storytellers even though they use very few words. They capture our imaginations with compelling settings, characters, and tensions. Their stories evoke emotions. So when you're telling a story, your top priority may not be on getting the details absolutely right or finding multiple sources for an event. Your investment is in having your readers and your "characters" connect. Whether or not you do it intentionally, when you're focusing on storytelling, you concentrate much more on the pacing of the story and the tension of the situation than you do on concepts like accuracy or truth.

A family storyteller has another handicap when it comes to getting the facts right: if you're telling a family story, chances are every family member has a different version of it. Once you've shared your version, someone in the family will most likely contact you with a correction. It's unavoidable. While compiling my own Treasure Chest, I wrote that my maternal grandpa had polio as a young man. When my aunt and uncle read the story, they quickly called me out on it. My uncle Joe, son of my grandpa, had never heard of his father having polio. My uncle remembered a story of grandpa having a different health crisis and being carried to the train to go to the nearest hospital but no memory of polio. My sister had also believed grandpa had polio, but when we put our heads together, neither one of us could remember our mother telling us that in so many words. When we consulted Aunt Ann, the family genealogist and the person who lived geographically closest to my grandparents, she had no record (or clear recall) of polio either, although she opined, "He had an illness in the 1920s which left him crippled. What else could it be?"

In this case, I decided to substitute truth for accuracy. I changed my sentence from, "Grandpa had polio in his youth that left him with a pronounced limp" to "Grandpa had health problems in his youth that left him frail."

The upside is that you're writing your memories about other people, not writing their biographies. The bar for accuracy is not nearly as high. Of course, the historian in your family might harass you a bit for more details, but he or she will connect to your writing.

Wearing the Memoirist's Hat

William Zinsser wrote, "Writers are the custodians of memory, and that's what you must become if you want to leave some kind of record of your life and of the family you were born into."[1] In compiling a Treasure Chest, you will leave a record of your past as you remember it for your children and other loved ones.

The words "as you remember it" are key. What we remember is our truth. The episodes and memories that we choose to commit to writing are a part of telling that truth. For instance, if you read my Treasure Chest, you would come to some overriding conclusions about me: My childhood wasn't perfect, but I was loved. Likewise, although I'm not the perfect parent, I love my kids immensely. Family and friends matter to me. My husband is a near-saint. These are my truths.

But I have smaller truths as my grandmother did before me. All her grandchildren were smart and beautiful. In my memory, my mother had a wonderful singing voice, but my mother never thought so. Who was right?

It doesn't matter who was right. My kids do not have their own memories of my mother singing to them. If I tell them that she sung lullabies to them and that I found her singing voice pleasant, that's really all that matters. The fact that she was self-conscious about her voice shouldn't be refuted either. We don't need an outside party to tell us who was right because we are living our own truths.

Memoir writing coach Matilda Butler makes a convincing argument that, because memory is not faultless, including the "emotional truth" of a story imbues it with an accuracy that a simple recantation of facts and events cannot:

> I think all of us have the sense of an emotional truth, versus some external reality out there. And I can tell you about, let's say, an argument with my son, and I can definitely give you the emotional truth of it. But will it be the exact words? No. How could it be? . . . Sometimes an emotional truth is even truer than if I went exactly line by line about what happened. Because, again, we are interpreting it in terms of what it meant to us.[2]

Your truths will come out as you write the stories of your past. When it comes to the details, you can ask your aunts, sisters, and brothers for them or even state that the details are fuzzy. However, when it comes down to it, telling the story in your memory is what will matter most to your loved ones.

1. William Zinsser, "How to Write a Memoir: Be yourself, speak freely, and think small," The American Scholar (Spring 2006), accessed July 18, 2013, http://theamerican-scholar.org/how-to-write-a-memoir/#.UehjxG32tEM.

2. Kendra Bonnett and Matilda Butler, "Interview on How to Write Memoirs—Part 5," William Victor, S.L. (2010), accessed December 5, 2011, http://www.creative-writing-now.com/how-to-write-memoirs.html.

MOMENTS VERSUS THE MOMENTOUS

Many of us have been children of relative peace, wealth, health, and happiness—not to mention relative obscurity. Our lives seem a bit short on momentous occasions, or at least what the rest of the world sees as momentous. Those who coach memoir writers disagree, insisting that every life is noteworthy, or worthy of the written word.

If that's true of a memoir, think how much more this wisdom applies to a Treasure Chest. Writing about your memories and writing a memoir are not the same. Memoirists write cohesive narratives about a part of their life or life journey. Bestselling memoirs are usually about life situations that are far from ordinary. A Treasure Chest, however, is not a memoir—at least not for most of us. We don't have to compose a chronicle of our life to give others insight into our makeup.

Though it can be autobiographical in nature, the writings a Treasure Chest contains do not necessarily integrate into one organized, comprehensive story. A Treasure Chest is not even necessarily in chronological order. Instead, it is a collection of memories and reflections that we believe are worthy of perpetuation. Obviously, experiences that shaped you and stand out in your memory warrant inclusion.

However, because each of our memories and experiences, regardless of how momentous they may be, have had some impact on the person we have become, less earthshaking events also belong in your collection. Memories, whether pivotal experiences or small moments we treasure, reflect our lives, the lessons we've learned, and the paths we've chosen. In many lives, everyday events are just as likely to serve as epiphanies and turning points as milestone events are. By writing about both the commonplace and life-changing events, we are leading our readers to the legacy we've decided to reveal.

The import of the pieces of memory we preserve and how clearly they mark our personal development will vary greatly. Most of us will have only a few memories that will mark the path of our life's journey like a towering rock cairn or a signpost. Many memories we write about might be more analogous to bread crumbs or broken twigs left on a trail—though they do not demarcate the overall journey as clearly, these crumbs give readers invaluable insight into our personality and character.

Of what are those bread crumbs, twigs, rock cairns, and signposts constructed? Of what are our memories made?

They're made of moments.

As time has continued its indefatigable march forward, some moments during the years have stood out more vividly than the rest. Even if our lives are short on momentous occasions, they are full of moments that were momentous to us. Every now and then, they're moments in the midst of the momentous. For instance, people in my parents' generation inevitably remember what they were doing when they learned of President John F. Kennedy's assassination. In my generation, we all know exactly where we were and what we were doing when we first learned of the September 11, 2001, attacks. The thing most deeply embedded in our memory isn't the general context of the historical event—it is of the moment of our realization.

Even less-historical moments are equally entrenched in our memory simply because they were consequential to us personally. These are precisely the moments that mark our journeys. For instance, I always knew, intellectually, that I would love my children, but I was unprepared for the overwhelming rush of love and devotion I felt in the moment that I first laid eyes on my son. In fact, I can remember that moment as if it were yesterday. That moment of love at first sight indelibly marked my entry into motherhood.

Frequently, our most cherished memories are moments in the midst of the mundane—the poignancies of the everyday. They might include a warm evening with a soft breeze in a beautiful setting with good friends, or your first sight of the Grand Canyon or the Chicago skyline. They might simply be a moment of happiness or heartbreak. They might include catching the look of pride in your father's eye. Such moments matter.

As you brainstorm and choose topics on which to reflect, be aware of the moments. Collected together, moments will be quite a treasure. Indeed, you can never be sure what will be most highly valued by those who receive your legacy of memories. One reader's trinket might be another's crown jewel.

Additional Tools:

Worksheet: Vivid Moments I Remember guides you as you brainstorm memorable moments.

My Turn: Fleeting, Enduring Memory tells the story of one of my most memorable moments.

Worksheet: Vivid Moments I Remember

Use this sheet to tickle your memory and jot down ideas about the things you might want to write about. No full sentences! This is just a bank for your ideas. Jot down just enough notes that you'll be able to come back to your ideas and develop them into stories.

Moments in which…

I felt especially proud:

I knew my life was headed in the right direction:

I knew what I was doing mattered:

I felt deeply connected to my family (parents, spouse, or children):

I felt deeply connected to nature or God:

I felt utterly loved:

I felt overwhelmed:

I was scared:

I knew what I was doing was right:

Childhood Moments

A typical happy moment:

A scary moment:

A moment when you felt close to a parent/grandparent:

A moment when you felt close to a sibling:

A moment of great accomplishment:

A moment of a great thrill:

A moment of great conflict:

What other moments stand out in your memory?

My Turn: Fleeting, Enduring Memory

My memory of my grandfather's funeral is reduced to a couple of fleeting moments. They are also enduring moments, for they define a father–daughter relationship.

I was seated beside my dad in the chapel. I'm sure my grandmother was on his other side, but I don't actually remember that. To the right of our family was a louvered divider, on the other side of which sat the majority of the congregation. Non-family-members could listen to the pastor's message spared from the sight of the family's naked grief.

In my favorite dress and trying to be good.

At seven, my feet didn't reach the floor, which is really kind of a metaphor. I didn't understand everything that was going on, only that everyone was sad and emotionally volatile. Born a peacemaker, I saw my role as finding ways to make people smile for a minute, or, at the very minimum, not to make anyone any sadder. This included dressing and behaving nicely.

In the background of my ephemeral memory, the smell of flowers borders on claustrophobic as a long prayer drones on. I'm carefully and quietly swinging my legs back and forth, staring down at my black patent-leather shoes, when a potential disaster strikes. My little purse clatters to the floor, presenting my seven-year-old peacemaker mind with a dilemma of epic proportions: Should I pick it up? Should I acknowledge that I dropped it? Was I in trouble for dropping it, especially during the prayer? Forty-two years later, I remember the panic building up in my throat and nausea sweeping over me. I stared down at the purse for what seemed like an eternity, finally deciding to do nothing. I snuck a peek at my father, hoping to see his eyes closed. Instead, I found him watching me with loving eyes. He winked at me and whispered, "Good girl!" before closing his eyes again.

With those two words, pride and relief replaced the panic.

So how do that wink and "Good girl!" now engrained in my memory, define our father–daughter relationship?

Now that my feet reach the floor, hopefully in more ways than one, I understand more of what was going on in my father's world that day. The only son had lost not only a wonderful, loving father; he was faced with dealing with his mentally ill mother from that point forward—alone. Additionally, his father was also revered by his church—a church Daddy had strayed from. Decades later, I found the sermon transcript; the cruelty of the message is still shocking. There was no mention in the funeral sermon of a loving or even a grieving son. There were only innuendos of not living up to the mold. The message, which should have been hopeful, warped the mourners' grief into a manifestation of selfishness. Failing to feel joyful at his father's entry into heaven was yet another sin.

In other words, during this moment, Daddy was grieving, scared, angry, and ostracized. It would have been completely understandable if he had shown irritation, ignored me, or been impatient with my neurotic purse dilemma. Instead, he reached out to me with love, patience, and understanding. Parent transcended self.

It wasn't my behavior that was tested in that moment; it was his.

He passed with flying colors.

PUTTING MEMORIES TO PAPER

Many memory collectors will find that getting started is perhaps the hardest part of their project. Ideas and thoughts seem elusive. The blank screen or blank piece of paper scares and intimidates us, paralyzing us into doing nothing. The harder we try, the more that paper seems to mock us. Suddenly unloading the dishwasher seems more worthwhile.

Now that you're organized, how do you start filling your Treasure Chest? How do you break through these roadblocks and start or restart when ideas stagnate?

Easy Does It

Another point of general agreement among writing resources is to start with what is easiest. The easiest stories to write are those about which you are passionate. Choose a topic that matters to you or a memory that you love to tell. A story that matters to you and also involves people who matter to you will be even more likely to facilitate the writing process. Once you've chosen a topic near and dear to your heart, you may find that your story writes itself. If not, there are a few other methods of getting your thoughts on paper.

Use a More Localized Brainstorm

We use brainstorming techniques to come up with ideas for topics, but they can also help bring story details to mind. Try quickly brainstorming the topic you've chosen. Grab a piece of paper and pencil and start jotting down notes. Include:

- what took place
- who was involved
- what you saw
- what you heard—including background noise

- what you smelled
- what you felt
- what, if anything, you learned

Create a Word Bank

If your story centers on a person, place, or event, it is often helpful to generate a word bank pertaining to your topic. You can move yourself gradually from those words that come easily (the facts) to the more difficult—analytical, sensory, and emotional details. You'll not only quickly home in on those words that are the best fit for what you want to write, thus getting your descriptive juices flowing, but you'll also find yourself more aptly portraying the meat of the matter: why it matters to you.

Up and Typing (or Writing)

On bookstore shelves or the Internet, you'll find a plethora of writing coaches offering exercises to improve your writing. I certainly recommend the ones provided in this book, but there are others that you are likely to find useful; in fact, you can find several suggestions in the Recommended Resources section at the end of this book. Practicing with writing exercises, reading about writing and style, and taking writing classes are also useful in improving your writing. But at some point, you will want to stop exercising, and start writing. Addressing this point, experts, teachers, and other writers usually come back to one salient piece of advice: just get started.

You may hate what you've written, but just breaking the barrier will help. You've started. Your writing will often improve as you continue, and the revision process will take care of the rest. Some writers suggest imagining that you're talking to a trusted friend as you type or write; others insist that it is more important for you to commune with the memory itself, allowing yourself to re-experience your surroundings, emotions, and thoughts. Regardless of how you do it, it's imperative that you break through that feeling of paralysis and put words onto paper or screen. You can't edit, revise, or rewrite a blank page.

Rewrite

Nobody's perfect. Even if you're an articulate, eloquent, and experienced writer, don't expect to avoid editing and rewriting. In fact, successful authors encourage it. Many of these writers are most comfortable letting their thoughts flow and getting the gist of their stories on paper.

Only afterward do they allow themselves to perfect their piece. This also prevents self-editing to interfere with the natural flow of ideas and narratives. If you practice this technique, the second or third time you read your piece, you may find grammatical errors, awkwardly worded sentences, and tangential information that you'd like to save for another time. You may also find places that you'd like to fill in with more detail or descriptions. During the rereading process, a better way to express a thought may occur to you.

There's another reason to give your writing time. Not only can you edit better after a little time has passed, but your memory may develop as well. Many of us find that, though the essence of our memories doesn't change, the details we remember and our feelings about events can change from time to time. As you approach your memory for the second time, you might have additional insights to add.

Keep Your Eye off the Prize

Keep your goal in mind. You are not writing for a Pulitzer Prize. Your goal is to preserve your memories. Likewise, your readers are not out to critique your style. They will be motivated by the need to connect with you and your past and not by the need to find literary genius.

Be yourself, too. Don't force yourself to follow someone else's style. Your readers want to connect with you, and if you write naturally, they'll be better able to do just that. We all want to write well, and we want our readers to enjoy our writing. There's nothing wrong with editing and perfecting your work, but don't let your concerns about literary style prevent you from achieving your goal of connecting with loved ones and leaving a legacy.

Especially if you find yourself bogged down and unable to write, tell your stories simply. Concentrate on communicating what you want to preserve, and worry less about literary excellence. Just imagine telling the stories to the people for whom you are writing. The real you will emerge from your memories.

Additional Tools:

Worksheet: Word Bank Exercise guides you as you build a word bank of descriptive words to use in your writing.

Worksheet: Word Bank Exercise

Use this worksheet to summon up a wealth of descriptive words to use in your writing. (You'll notice no colors are included. Colors are the easiest to recall; we're looking a little deeper here.) Think of a favorite place in nature. As you recall it, allow your mind to recall the sounds, smells, mood, temperature, and so forth. Write down as many descriptive words as you can.

Appearance: (clear, sloping, gnarled, dark, steep, rolling, and so on)

Sounds: (gurgle, crackle, whiney, buzz, chatter, and so forth)

Smells: (such as acrid, fresh, flowery, and so on)

Mood: (for example, exhilarating, peaceful, holy, isolated, and so forth)

Temperature: (such as sweltering, frigid, mild, and so on)

Part 2

Keeping Track of Ideas

Ideas can pop up so quickly that you might struggle to get them down on paper before you lose track of them. Creativity doesn't just flow; it overflows. That's a good thing. Solutions for keeping track of ideas are straightforward, and they let you save ideas for those times when there's a metaphorical drought.

Often, saving ideas for later also lets those ideas develop, much like a sauce on the stove top. Your memories, like flavors, will blend and develop into something the whole family will enjoy.

Just as your Treasure Chest will reflect your creativity and need for structure, so will your system for keeping up with ideas. Obviously, I strongly recommend keeping your brainstorming sheets and using the idea bank described in the next session. However, your personality is going to determine whether you keep up with your ideas on a computer file, in a notebook, or with color-coded index cards. The important thing is to have a system that works for you.

IDEA BANK

One system for keeping up with passing thoughts and ideas so you can come back to them regularly is an idea bank. An idea bank is a notebook, file, or electronic document where you store the glimmers of ideas that you have. Don't think of it as a glorified list but rather as a safe-deposit box with no fees. You can also think of it as a nursery for your ideas—a place where ideas are protected and nurtured. It's a simple tool, but it can be of great value to a writer. Whenever you feel ready to come back to your ideas to develop them into writing pieces, they'll be there, safe and sound. Whatever you decide to call your idea bank, start one of your own.

These storage devices really come in handy on those days when your imagination falls flat. Some days you'll have much to deposit in your bank. Remember, however, that you're not trying to accumulate a life's savings—don't hesitate to make withdrawals!

To get you going, the next section of this book presents a starter idea bank. It's a list of ideas, many of which are based on my grandmother's Treasure Chest, for you to use as inspiration. As you try each prompt and exercise, you'll be contributing to your Treasure Chest and documenting your priceless family memories.

Enjoy! As you work your way through each of the following topics, immerse yourself in the memories and enjoy the process of connecting with your past and your loved ones.

"THINGS I WANT
TO REMEMBER"

LEAVING SNAPSHOTS FROM YOUR PAST

One essay my grandmother left that I truly love is entitled "Things I Want to Remember." In it, she briefly dwelt on her memories of each of her children. What makes this such a gem, however, isn't simply a mother's descriptions of her growing children, but rather the way in which she allows her readers access to those scenes in her memory as if she were leaving a snapshot in time. Rather than merely describing what each child looked like, my grandmother gives us insight into what they were like. She gives us a snapshot in time of each of them, describing their gestures, expressions, and actions in a very small setting. This not only gives me a better connection to my grandmother, but to my mother, aunt, and uncles as well.

My aunt Nancy is a case in point. We knew from old photographs what she looked like in her youth, but Grandma's description gave her a new dimension. I knew the mother of five, capable night nurse, devout Southern Baptist, and woman that knew her own mind. But I was taken aback by my grandmother's snapshot of my aunt: a little girl eager to please and relishing a close relationship with her uncle. This was not how I would have characterized the aunt I knew.

I've come to understand that the snapshot my grandmother left of my aunt is true today—either it remains true or perhaps it is true again. Aunt Nancy suffers from Alzheimer's and isn't very keenly aware of those around her. Although she remains pleasant and friendly to me, she ceased to recognize me almost a decade ago. She lives close to my cousin and spends much of her time good-naturedly sweeping and tidying up. With the passage of time, or perhaps despite it, in many ways she is the little girl her mother described—cheerful, eager to please, and trusting of her guardians.

Such literary snap-shots can also be used to preserve a smaller picture or part of a picture. Sometimes there are things we want to remember that aren't quite a story—things like gestures, habits, sayings, or idiosyncrasies. For example, I don't want to forget how my youngest used the words *lane* for *street* and *persons* for *people*. These details work very well within this Things I Want to Remember concept and can be included as a separate point or as part of the snapshot you are providing for your readers.

Try leaving a snapshot of your past. It

My mother posed for her mother. The photograph is torn, but the memory is still intact.

doesn't have to be more than a few lines. Think of a time or a person in time that you always want to remember. As you replay scenes from your past in your mind, make note of gestures, expressions, emotions, hopes, and intentions. When you write about it, describe it terms of the actions taking place and the feelings experienced as the shot was snapped.

Additional Tools:

Worksheet: Things I Want to Remember helps you recall the things you want to remember about a loved one.

My Turn: Things I Want to Remember about Hazel provides some snapshots of my inspiration—my grandmother.

Worksheet: Things I Want to Remember

About: _____ (name)

Choose someone about whom you might want to write. Use this sheet to brainstorm and develop your thoughts about him or her.

Physical attributes that you want to remember:

Hair color and texture:

Eye Color:

Skin tone:

Laugh lines (or not):

Height:

Other attributes: (big hands, funny ears, easy smile, farmer's tan, and so on. *Be sure to include ages. You'll think you'll remember, but you won't.*)

Situations

School together:

Jokes:

Pranks:

Athletics together:

Projects together:

Raising kids together:

Raising Cain together:

Embarrassing situations:

Touching or moving situations:

Childhood antics: (games, snowball fights, hangouts, and so forth)

Other Situations:

Mannerisms about this person that you want to remember:

Habits:

Quirks:

Figures of Speech:

General Nature:

Eccentricities:

Gifts and talents:

My Turn: Things I Want to Remember
about Hazel Savoy Crymes a.k.a. Grandma Crymes

—*Her laugh:* Being around Grandma was like riding a wind of happiness.

—*Her love:* Grandma made each of us feel special. When we visited, photos of cousins were hidden away while my sister's and mine were prominently displayed.

—*Her biscuits:* Not the taste, for that I have, alas, forgotten, but the making of them. When Grandma made biscuits, all baking surfaces, her ever-smiling face, and even her dress were dusted with flour.

—*Her writings:* Through them I connect with a woman full of wonder, grief, hopes, and fears—in short, a friend has come to stand where only a grandmother stood before.

—*Her dialogue with God:* Her daily walk and talks with God included not only prayers, but laments and questions as well. I will never forget her chiding God for his "taking" of "young" (aged sixty) Charles Powell when she herself was so ready to go.

—*Her rose-colored glasses:* Grandma had an incredible and never-failing ability to look past wrongdoings and shortcomings and to continue to find good and to love. This was, perhaps, her greatest blessing, and it was surely the best gift she passed on to her daughter, my mother, Ellen.

EASY SNAPSHOTS IN TIME

The Holiday Letter

This idea is so easy that it almost seems like cheating. Simply include a copy of an annual holiday letter in your Treasure Chest. It couldn't be easier. What an effective way of giving yourself and others a snapshot of yourself and your family in time! That is, unless you write the dreaded brag letter. Look back over the Christmas letters that you sent three to five years ago and see if they don't take you back. These letters will give you a snapshot in time as you remember the things that were important to you at the time you wrote it.

If you don't have an old Christmas or other holiday letter to draw from, try using the included worksheet to re-create or create one. Remember to be yourself. Don't use language that your recipients couldn't imagine you using normally. If your creativity hits a wall, consider using and alternative approach such as:

Newspaper-style newsletter with articles about (or by) each family member

The year in pictures—using a couple of representative pictures to tell the year's stories

A poem, whether rhyming or not

Alternate voice, such as writing from the viewpoint of child, new pet, appliance, or other household observer.

If you do have one or more past newsletters, just for fun, try annotating one. Note the ways in which your life has changed or remains much the same. How has your perspective on life and previous events changed? This will not only be a fun exercise—it will make excellent reading for family members as well.

Additional Tools:

Worksheet: Writing an Annual Holiday Letter guides you through writing an annual letter.

My Turn: Christmas 2004 Letter describes a year-end under construction.

Worksheet: Writing an Annual Holiday Letter

If you don't have an old holiday letter to use (or don't like the one you have), you can create or re-create one. Here are some ideas. Jot down notes about the ones that you'd like to use.

High Points/Low Points of the Year:

Graduations:

Change in schools:

New jobs:

Change in family status: (adoption, divorce, remarriage, exchange student, and so on)

New pet:

Sickness, or death in family:

New toys: (car, boat, and so forth)

Sports activities or championships:

Community involvement: (ran for school board, PTA president, active volunteer, and such)

Children's activities:

Theatre or dance productions:

The facts

What fills your days?

What makes your heart sing?

What things in your life make you feel good? What things make you feel proud?

What are your wishes for your letter recipients?

How are you going to make your letter visually appealing? Do you have photos of events you've written about or of family members? *Insert clip art and photos, or scan and insert hand-drawn illustrations or other handcrafted materials.*

My Turn: Christmas 2004 Letter

Season's Greetings and Salutations!

No hint of a lie, I almost wrote "Greetings and Hallucinations." We're not sure whether we're coming or going this year. As we drive towards South Carolina with the car loaded to the gills with presents, kids, kid paraphernalia, dog, and dog paraphernalia, we wonder what Santa and his elves will think on Christmas Eve at the sight of our home.

Yes, after six years of deliberation, the Hedgecocks actually, finally made a decision. (We're sure those of you close to the process would like even more emphasis on the finally; sorry, we don't travel with a thesaurus.) Our ranch house, formerly 28' x 60' (no, the fact that those are the exact dimensions of a double-wide is *not* lost on us) is undergoing construction to get a new kitchen and eating area addition, change our current kitchen to a dining room and mud room, and to make the back bedroom a "master." A master has his own bathroom, but in this family, it's the missus that's dying to stop sharing a bathroom with two growing boys.

On Christmas Eve, Santa will find the chimney, which leads to the downstairs living area (three hundred square feet that is now family room, office, music room, dining room, and foyer), is duct-taped closed. The front door would be an alternative if we had one. Since a gas line has to move before a door goes in, the builder is waiting for word from on high (a.k.a. Consumers Energy) before they put one in. If Santa's elves are good with a crowbar, there are only two nails and a sheet of OSB board between them and the interior of the home. We'd recommend roof parking to the reindeer since that's the one part of the job that's finished. The driveway and yard are littered with construction hazards, including lumber, sawhorses, a huge dirt pile, an overfilled dumpster, and stone that's waiting to be reused. If the elves scavenged through the dumpster, they might find treasures not seen for the last fifty years. The only Christmas lights we have up are the reindeer perched on the dirt pile in the back. We had plans to put lights on Scotty's porta-potty in the front yard, but the two-degree weather just before we left put a kibosh on that, although one neighbor offered to decorate it with dreidels. (That's all she has at her house.) We hope she does.

Other than that, you can sum up our lives as approximately x+1, where x=our lives this time last year. Nathaniel, now in 5th grade, is still doing great in school; now wears glasses; loves music, reading, writing, and tennis; and is passionate about soccer. Joshua is in the 3rd grade; seems to be good at everything except getting along with Nathaniel; also plays soccer (different club than Nathaniel—this way I can play super soccer mom and get them to simultaneous practices that take place nine miles apart); and keeps us all entertained with his slightly offbeat humor. Matt is still with the same company but now calls on Ford. So far, this means less travel, which makes the rest of us happy. I'm approximately the same—still playing soccer, managing soccer teams, and running the science fair and Junior Great Books (a reading program that fosters analytical thinking) for their school. I'm still running from doctor to doctor to deal with all my little maladies, but in general, I'm happy, and the addition is wearing but not as wearing as we expected.

We'd love to hear your updates too. As we come to the end of our eleven-hour trip, we feel the stress of the everyday evaporate, replaced by the excitement of time with those who love us most and the hope of Christmas. We hope this letter finds each of you healthy and happy and that the Peace of Christmas visits your household too.

Merry Christmas and best wishes for the coming New Year!

REFLECTIONS ON A DEAR FRIEND

Family members are not the only ones who play a starring role in our emotional and spiritual well-being. Friends can become as close as family, especially if we live far away from our biological relatives. There are times—when the nest is empty or when family is no longer with us—that good friends fill the gaps. Many of us have friends that have stood by us throughout the years, sharing good times, bringing meals, and mopping up tears in times of sorrow. They are fixtures in our lives.

My grandmother wrote a loving poem in honor of her friend Martha Ellen Clark Gee entitled "Ellen of Virginia." Much of her poem had to do with how heartbreaking it would be if her friend ever left Virginia. For my mother, also named Ellen, this was a very moving piece. She had always harbored doubts about leaving her home state of Virginia and living so far from her parents. She was gratified to see that when she wasn't able to be with her mother, a dear friend was.

Writing about your feelings for a friend gives loved ones (your readers) insight into your development, regardless of whether it was a childhood or an adult friendship. That doesn't mean that you need to write about every friend you have, but consider writing about those friendship experiences that have helped mold you.

Another reason to write about friends is the simple fact that our loved ones tend to love the people we love. We can develop affection for a near stranger based only on their relationship to someone we love. For example, my mother had a friend named Nancy Green. I've never met Nancy, but I have a deep fondness for her. This grows not only out of the fact that she shared a childhood with my mother, but also from their shared passion for art and the fact that they managed to stay close through five decades of living far away from one another. Likewise, I have strong connections to some of the youth for whom my mother advocated as a child protection worker. I never knew their names, but because my mom cared so deeply about them, I think about them from time to time and pray that they have found their paths to happiness. Before you start deliberating about which friend is "best," realize that this is *not* a competition or ranking. It's simply your feelings about someone and the role they play or have played in your life.

Try writing down your memories of—and reflections on—a dear friend. It can rhyme, be in simple prose, or be an essay. You can use a geographical reference like my grandmother did, but that is optional. The point of this exercise is to convey some sense of this person to your readers.

As you use the included brainstorming sheet, think back on your friends and choose one or more about whom you'd like to write. You can choose the mood and the tone. Memorialize hilarious moments of friendships, loyalties shared for a lifetime, or relationships that pulled you through when the rest of your life seemed to fall apart.

Additional Tools:

Worksheet: Reflections on a Dear Friend helps you determine what you want to communicate about a special friend.

My Turn: Laura of Laurens is my reflection on a friend I dearly miss.

Worksheet: Reflections on a Dear Friend

About: _____

Date: _____

Use this worksheet to brainstorm some things you want to remember about a special friend.

Physical attributes that you want to remember: (hair color, eye color, and so on)

If you want, include a geographical location:

Personality attributes you share: (compassionate, funny, happy, warm, friendly, shy)

Personality attributes that complement yours:

How you met:

Big events that drew you close:

Your dreams, hopes, or wishes for this friend:

The bonds you share: (shared childhood, college roommates, raising children together, work, and so forth)

- Why you treasure your friend: (This is actually the hardest to articulate. It may be highly private, ranging from unwavering support to making you laugh when you need it most.)

My Turn: Laura of Laurens

My friend Laura on my wedding day.

Sparkling blue eyes and big white smile,
That's how I'll remember you.
Laura, Miss Laurens
Blonde hair pulled back, casually beautiful,
Alternatively, stunning when you wanted to be.
Sparkling blue eyes and big white smile,
That's how I'll remember you.

Your beauty was a part of you
Though not completely at home with it,
Fearful that it would be a divide between you and others,
Yet treasuring it, realizing its fleeting nature
You worked harder than the rest,
Ran faster, practiced more, yet always with
Sparkling blue eyes and big white smile,
That's how I'll remember you.

Open heart, tender heart,
Living in the moment—picking daisies
Living for the future—always improving somehow

Using your every gift and talent
Never needing to improve on friendship, always with
Sparkling blue eyes and big white smile,
That's how I'll remember you.

When I heard what had happened,
I never doubted you for a minute.
"She'll be in wheelchair races in Sydney.
Nothing can stop our Laura." I could see your
Open heart, determined white smile
Sparkling blue eyes and big white smile,
That's how I'll remember you.

Fast friends, sharing a name,
Sharing a past, sharing our dreams,
Sharing laughs, sharing friends.
No one could come between us—certainly not some drunk
But suddenly, crushing words: "Damage too severe."
"No brain activity. None from the scene"
Runner's body no match for speeding steel and glass; yet
Sparkling blue eyes and big white smile,
That's how I'll remember you.

Gone from us, yet you continued to share.
Marathoner's lungs too battered, but liver, kidney, cornea, skin
Gave life and hope to others.
I close my eyes and force the ugly images away—
Open heart, tender heart,
Sparkling blue eyes, big white smile,
That's how I remember you.

Written in memory of Laura Sullivan Griffin, who was killed by a drunk and stoned driver while jogging in Charleston, South Carolina, on January 17, 1996.

KIDDIE CORNER

Our kids are an integral part of our lives, and it would be impossible to tell the story of our lives without including them. Indeed, future generations who come to know and love your children as adults will enjoy the connection to the child they never knew.

Without even trying, when you write about different topics, you will inevitably cover how much your kids mean to you, how much you care about them, and how much they enrich your life. Naturally, stories centering on your memories of your children will also need a place in your Treasure Chest.

With all the material they provide us with, it becomes difficult to write anything less than an entire tome about them. How do you hone the essence of your growing or grown child into a Treasure Chest entry (or two or three)?

An Abridged Anti-Brag Letter

I know everyone hates brag letters—that's where this alternative comes in. Think of it as an anti-brag letter. This is not a litany of superlatives or, heaven forbid, reasons why your child is better than the rest. *Without naming their accomplishments*, think and write about why you're proud of your kids and the individuals into which they are developing.

This approach does require a modicum of care. Don't just abridge the length; make sure you curb the bragging as well. Keep your readers in mind and remember that most of us are incredibly proud of our kids, regardless of their level of achievement. Avoid intimating that your children are in any way more precious than your readers' children are. Keep your subject in mind too. Ironically, kids that know they are academically or athletically gifted are accustomed to receiving accolades in their area of expertise. They crave validation and appreciation for their more subtle achievements,

71

such as compassion, clearheadedness, and responsibility.

Ideally, when family and friends read your memories, they'll be inspired to write their own thoughts about their children. This is a wonderful way to have meaningful and honest conversations about parenting and child rearing and, if enough time has passed, the antics of your children. It's an opportunity to bond. This is another reason to avoid bragging: you don't want to introduce competitiveness into the mix.

How do you, your child's biggest fan, write about him or her without bragging? With a little finesse, it becomes easy. By all means include the fact that your son or daughter was valedictorian or a Division I athlete. Just take a little care in *how* you mention it. Compare the following sentences: "We were so proud that George graduated #1 in his class." "Thrilled as he was to graduate at the top of his class, George was terrified at the prospect of giving the valedictorian speech." Admittedly, the second sentence took longer to craft. It does, however, tell us more about George's personality. It's worth the editing effort.

Think about the people that will eventually read what you've written. Have you provided them with what they really want to know about your child? Have you given them a feel for his or her character? Is your child shy or gregarious? Creative or thoughtful? Daredevil or cautious? The natural leader or a more docile follower? Keep these things in mind when selecting which photos to include as well; look for images that capture your little one's character. The more your readers can envision what your child is like, the more likely they are to feel a bond.

Writing about your children's passions and how they demonstrate them is a great way to show without bragging. Are they compassionate, self-possessed, funny, or a walking encyclopedia on Kingdom Animalia? Do they draw and paint at every opportunity or attempt to take apart and rebuild any mechanical object in the house? Does he sleep with a basketball or stash candy under his bed? Does she not go out in public without the correct underwear or "rescue" long-dead animals? Even though the interests of early childhood are often passing, they reveal a lot about the little personhood in progress. As children age, these early interests might translate into a love for music, drama (hopefully on stage), or sports. Your children don't even have to be particularly good at the activity about which they're passionate for it to be worth mentioning. The things that they love to do give great insights into their personalities.

If my mother had kept a Treasure Chest, she'd undoubtedly stress my love for animals and include the day I tried to "rescue" an injured shrew, which resulted in my inability to perform in my guitar recital. My friend Beth would include how her toddler used to "free" other female toddlers of their hair bows, never comprehending the trail of tears left along her revolutionary route. Such little episodes reveal not only the developing character of the child but the parent–child relationship as well.

A Day in the Life

Alternatively, you could highlight some of the mundane moments of life. Sometimes everyday activities best convey the small personality in bloom. Consider describing a typical afternoon or outing. What kind of things do you do? How do the kids relate to each other? Do they have special or unusual friendships? Such little episodes can also reveal the child's developing character and the parent-child relationship. If you'd like, you can leave out extraneous details like unmade beds, cheerios under furniture, and the like.

Antics

Our kids' antics can be more articulate than innumerable pages of description. Remember how there was a whole television show based on the premise that "kids say the darnedest things"? The show is no longer on, but kids are still providing tons of subject matter for writers. Think of how many times you've recounted a story about your kids and received the response, "You've *got* to write that one down!"

Well, go ahead and do it! Write down some of your kids' more memorable moments, adorable or not—and don't forget to note the date and add photos when you can.

Though they do have their adorable moments, kids aren't always adorable. There's no question that our kids can be, and in most cases have been, an embarrassment to us at one time or another. Some of us have a couple of stories that we hold close, telling our kids that if they're not careful, they'll hear them again at their weddings. Others of us love recounting them at every get-together. And it doesn't have to be just kids that are the subject of these blackmail stories. You might be telling on your uncle, your neighbor, or even on yourself. These are the perfect stories for a Treasure Chest because they're the ones we end up retelling at family reunions anyway.

Most of these stories are funny to all involved a couple of months or years after the event. However, if the subject of the story will be truly embarrassed or if telling the story will damage your relationship with your child, skip it. There are plenty of other things to write about.

Start Writing

Try recounting that embarrassing story involving the minister, the lost key to the city, or the visiting business partner. Don't hesitate to let your sense of humor shine through.

Additional Tools:

Worksheet: Brainstorming about a Taste of the Growing-up Years helps you brainstorm about your child's interests and personality.

Worksheet: Brainstorming about Your Child's Antics helps you identify antics to share with loved ones

My Turn: Scientific Method to His Madness? relates the story of one of my son's so-called good ideas.

Worksheet: Brainstorming about a Taste of the Growing-up Years

About:_____ (Child's Name)

Jot down ideas about the things you might want to write about, both out-standing and mundane. No full sentences! This is just a bank for your ideas. You may make copies for your personal use to brainstorm about more than one child.

Personality as a Young Child

Look at the word choices below. Jot down whatever thoughts come to mind. Some might be a story in themselves; others will be the flavoring in other things you write. If you child is old enough, note whether his or her personality has changed with age.

Exuberant or careful?

Spontaneous or a planner?

Extremely active, active, calm, or sedentary?

Creative and artistic or little engineer at work?

Like to get dirty or clean freak? Willing to touch gooey things?

Special abilities or disabilities? (such as fine motor skills, speed, or memory)

Elementary School Interests:

Academic: (interests, favorite subjects, and so on)

Art: (Hint: A digital camera can help you capture kids' art digitally.)

Creative writing:

Chorus, choir, or instrumental music:

Reading:

Science or Science Fair:

Sports:

Friendships:

Favorite toys:

Other:

Junior High and High School Interests:

Academic: (interests, favorite subjects, AP classes, study habits, and so forth)

Art: (Hint: Use a digital camera.)

Creative writing:

Choral or instrumental ensembles:

Leadership:

Science or Science Fair:

School sports:

Friendships:

Other: (hobby groups, after-school projects, and so on)

Home, church, and community:

Relationships with siblings:

Helping around the house:

Service projects:

Drama roles:

Confirmation or Bar Mitzvah:

Vocal or instrumental music lessons, choirs, or ensembles:

Club and city-league sports teams:

Stages: (for example, drama queen or goth)

Worksheet: Brainstorming about your Child's Antics

I hope that by now you've brainstormed a little about your child's growing-up years. Doing that first will help get the memories flowing. Now we'll go back through some of those categories and see if any funny, sweet, or tender memories spring to light. Under each category, various situations are listed. As thoughts occur to you, add your own. Jot down just enough notes that you can come back and use this list as an idea bank.

Preschool Years

Situations in church or synagogue: (things said or done during the children's sermon, services, or church school)

Childishly honest observations: (things said upon meeting or observing someone who looked different; honest assessments of family members' looks.)

Situations with playmates: (partners in crime, jealousy, competitiveness, loyalty, observations about friends)

Messes and attempts to hide the evidence: (needs no explanation; they've all done it.)

Elementary School

School: (situations with teachers, administrators, oral reports, getting in trouble, and things blurted out in front of visitors)

Tattletale: (things told to teachers or other adults about their parents or other kids)

Creative writing: (things written down or on display)

Group projects: (were they ever less than the perfect cooperative force?)

Junior High or High School

This is like your Elementary School brainstorming exercise, only now with a mouthy pre-teen or teenage edge.

School: (situations with teachers, administrators, oral reports, getting in trouble, things blurted out in front of visitors)

Creative writing: (things written down or on display)

Group projects:

Sports: (comedic moments on the field, with coaches, and so on)

Home, Church, and Community

Relationships with siblings: (squabbles, wrestles, grudges, and escapades in general)

Siblings as cohorts in crime: (the dreaded "I have an idea . . ." to which someone should have yelled, "No!")

Drama roles: (when life went off-script—not necessarily related to a theatre role)

Confirmation or Bar Mitzvah: (nice speeches, funny or poignant moments)

Ensembles: (ever have the "my child is the only one doing it right" experience?)

Sports teams: (bloopers, accidents, situations with coaches, fouls, penalties, and cards)

My Turn: Scientific Method to His Madness?

We intentionally teach kids scientific method so that they will begin to think analytically and experiment in real life. So why wasn't I proud when twelve-year-old Nathaniel employed the scientific method on his own?

You be the judge. Here's how the experimental process went down:

Step 1: Define the problem

Son's thoughts: I wonder . . .

Mom's thoughts: I'm pretty sure he skipped this one. There wasn't a problem. I'm not even sure there was any thinking. The popcorn popper does an excellent job of popping popcorn.

Step 2: Develop a hypothesis and explain your reasoning

Son's thoughts: If things heat better under pressure, I bet I can pop popcorn better by putting the kernels under pressure as they heat.

Mom's thoughts: I'll give him this one. The hypothesis was reasonable.

Step 3: Design your experiment

Son's thoughts: I'll put some popcorn kernels in mom's soup thermos and tighten the lid. I'll then put the thermos in the toaster oven see if they pop.

Mom's thoughts, had she had an opportunity to voice them at the time: Noooooooooooooo!

Step 4: Record data and observations

Son's thoughts: Okay, it's heating. I'll go watch TV until the oven goes ding. Hmmm. It's starting to smell funny. What? Smoke alarm? Uh-oh. Mom's going to notice the smoke alarm going off.

What's that smell? (Peeking in the toaster oven) This looks very bad. I'm very screwed.

Mom's thoughts: What's on fire? What's that smell? Naaaaaaaaaaaaate! . . . My toaster oven! My thermos! My newly renovated, smoke-covered, stinky kitchen!

Step 5: Publish & Explain your Conclusions

Son: Methodology needs some tweaking, but when it all cooled down, I saw that one kernel had popped. Hypothesis confirmed.

Cost of experiment:

$70 for replacing toaster oven and thermos

Time—I had to clean everything up and get dragged to Kohl's to buy the new toaster oven and thermos

Being right even though I'm in trouble—priceless

Mom's thoughts: [not printable]

TRAVELING DOWN MEMORY LANE

"Come with Me back to my Childhood Home"

My grandmother in front of her home.

"Come with Me Back to My Childhood Home" was the title that my grandmother used when she wrote about one of the homes of her childhood. She was feeling ill and used her writing as a distraction, taking her reader back in place and time.

The dwellings in which we spend our childhood years take on prominent roles in our memories. Perhaps the layout of our homes dictated much of the rhythm of our daily lives as we grew up, or perhaps the plasticity of the developing child's mind causes the memories made there to be so deeply chiseled. Like my grandmother, I too have thought back on my childhood home during a fever. I remember waking in the night and trying to navigate my way in the dark to the bathroom. I soon ran into a dresser. In my somnolent state, I was navigating from my childhood bed to the bathroom in the home of my youth. That's how much a part of me that house was—and still is.

In my family, we tended to live in one unpretentious house for decades. As a result, many memories revolve around the same physical building and surrounding neighborhood. If you grew up in multiple homes, you might not have the same indelible imaging of your parents' home on your memory. Your "childhood home" might be your grandparents' or aunt's home, your school, or your community center. Similarly, if your family tended to move more often, you probably have bits and pieces of different homes that stand out in your recollections.

Regardless, the fact is that the place or places you lived were a part of growing up and were the setting where the "forming" of your formative years took place. That's the way it was for my grandmother. She was raised by the extended family, spending months or years in whoever's home had an extra bed. Far from giving her less to write about, Grandma's love for these places shines through her writing.

For most of us, home was the place we felt safe, loved, and free to form ourselves. Even if your growing-up place cannot be painted as idyllic (and I'm not advocating revising your past), your memories of it will interest the generations coming after you and will deepen the connections you have with family members that share your memories of the place.

Every story is better with a well-described setting. Was your home the setting of important family events like reunions? Were children born in your home? Leave your readers with some impressions of your childhood home, especially if it is no longer in the family or is far away. Describe not only the physical characteristics of your home but also the sensations of the place. What were you likely to hear, smell, and feel? As you complete the included exercises, take your readers for a stroll down memory lane, up your front walk, and on a tour of your home.

Additional Tools:

Worksheet: Brainstorming about a Childhood Home will assist you as you brainstorm your memories about a particular place.

Worksheet: Word Bank Exercise for Your Childhood Home will help you build a word bank of rich descriptive words about your childhood home.

Writing Guide for "Come with Me to My Childhood Home" guides you as you invite your readers into the past to tour your childhood home.

My Turn: Come with Me Back to My Childhood Home—Excerpt takes you back to my South Carolina home.

Worksheet: Brainstorming about a Childhood Home

Jot down ideas about the things you might want to write about. No full sentences! This is just a bank for your ideas.

Place: (city, state, country)

Neighborhood type: (urban, suburban, rural)

Time period:_____

Exterior

Style and size of house or building:

Special features of this dwelling:

Lot or property size:

Memorable trees or plants:

Outdoor structures: (such as barn, shed, play structure or tree house)

Specific memories associated with the yard or the home's exterior: (sat on that stoop, climbed this tree, and so forth)

Interior

Briefly describe the layout:

Additions, renovations, and other layout changes:

Architectural or decorative style:

Level of cleanliness: (immaculate, cluttered, or otherwise)

Rooms

Briefly describe the kitchen and who was in it most often:

Describe where you slept:

Describe where you played:

Describe the area where family gathered or where holidays were celebrated:

If there were quirky or secret rooms, definitely include them:

Associations

Describe the sounds (or sights or smells) that you associate with this home:

Describe the emotions you associate with this home:

Worksheet: Word Bank Exercise for Your Childhood Home

Think about the home you want to describe. After each prompt, fill in words that describe that home.

Exterior appearance: (such as bleak, forbidding, cavernous, tiny, homey)

Interior appearance: (for example, clean, cluttered, flashy, hospitable, light)

Furnishings: (comfy, chic, elegant, mismatched, masculine, dingy, and so forth)

Activity level: (bustling, lively, quiet, and so on)

Mood: (such as angry, cheerful, depressing, cozy, safe)

Sounds or sound level: (boisterous, oppressive silence, buzzing, and so on)

Smells: (aromatic, earthy, moldy; include pet smells and other aromas and so forth)

Writing Guide for "Come with Me to My Childhood Home"

Use this guide to start drafting your memories of you childhood home on a sheet of paper or in a word processing application. As you read each prompt, think back and write down some notes about the home you are remembering as if you were taking a loved one on a walk-through.

Describe how you will approach the home. What do you see as you walk or drive up?

Now enter the house and begin to walk through. Describe what you see and remember.

Start walking to the room where you slept. Be sure to pause to listen to the sounds you remember as you begin your description.

Move on to describe the rooms where you played.

Describe where family holidays were celebrated.

Sum up your tour with your feelings about this place.

My Turn: Come with Me to My Childhood Home—Excerpt

Note: This excerpt is based on my completed writing guide. You'll notice that I also experimented with writing in a more childish voice.

Come back with me to a simpler time and see a place where I thrived— my childhood home. I'll tell you about the house and about our lives in it.

It's in Spartanburg, South Carolina. We're right off a major road, just a quarter mile or so down from Woodland Heights Elementary School. It's down two steep hills. Had it ever snowed much here, those hills would have been great for sledding because no one used to drive in the snow. We used to ride bikes with no hands and no feet down the hill, sometimes with disastrous results.

With no traffic to speak of, we could also play tennis or ride bikes in the street. If anyone had a big box, we'd tear it open and use it to slide down the hill next door and across the street into the empty lot. Once we used a refrigerator box and didn't even open it flat. We'd just roll around in there. The empty lot was also popular for its awesome mulberry tree— great for eating and climbing.

My childhood home.

The hall back to my room takes a dogleg bend. Going straight from the den leads you to the blue bathroom. Guess what color its walls are? Fixtures? You got it! It was the scene of the crime in which I lost face and trustworthiness in my mother's eyes for a while. Sick of my sister bossing me around, I took soap and wrote her name on the blue striped wallpaper, trying to get her in trouble. (I was probably there waiting for someone to bring me toilet paper; we were always out.) My parents could tell a

87

six-year-old's writing from an eight-year-old's. Busted!

Back in my room, you could often hear the TV, Mom laughing, and the dog barking (or howling if he heard a siren). My room was across the hall from Mom and Dad's and was painted a bright yellow. There was a big multicolor rug over the hardwood floor and a flat canopy over the bed with matching yellow-and-white gingham buffoon things for the bedposts. Mom made them out of bedsheets. With two windows on the front wall and one on the side, there was a lot of light. Sometimes, on quiet nights, you could hear trains.

I always liked my room. I could feel creative there—and comforted when I was unhappy. I shared my bed with the cats (and sometimes Pogo if we were sneaky) as well as my countless stuffed animals. When Däna was older, her band would practice in the basement right under me. Talk about disturbing the peace! Of course, that was second to Daddy's snoring and talking in his sleep. He was like a human freight train with his snoring. He'd talk too, but mostly agreed with people in his dreams, saying "Uh-huh, uh-huh, uh-huh, mmm." If you wanted something, it would always be tempting to ask Daddy for it while he was sleeping.

If we played inside, we'd mostly play in the basement, where we had a veritable Barbie empire along with a Ping-Pong table, loads of games, and an ugly brown sectional sofa. More often than not, though, we'd play outside. We had a big backyard that sloped down toward the house (always an issue during flash floods) bordered by pines. Sometimes we'd play kickball back here or hang upside down on the jungle gym, but it was actually more fun to explore the fields behind our house or the woods across the street, where there was better tree climbing and a creek.

We didn't have any relatives close by, so holidays were just the four of us. What we lacked in numbers, we made up for in enthusiasm. There were a lot of crafts and decorating at Christmas, though actually cooking the meals sometimes resulted in squabbles. On Christmas day, the living room, where the tree was, was off-limits at first. We'd go straight into the den and explore the stockings. Only after we'd enjoyed a less-than-nutritious breakfast of Dunkin' Donuts from the neighboring city of Greenville did we go in to see what Santa had left and open our presents.

When relatives did visit, we would gather in the kitchen, although sheer numbers might force us to eat in the dining room. When Aunt Nancy, Uncle Max, and our cousins came, Däna and I would play with the boys outside during the day, but late evenings were for girl talk in the kitchen with my cousin Sue Ellen and Aunt Nancy. Because the Hughes were teetotalers, Mom made Daddy move his beer to the fridge downstairs. He would sneak one with him into the shower. They probably thought him a very clean man because he showered for so long.

Though not a mansion, this house was a big, friendly, comfortable place to grow up. Like us, it has suffered aesthetically as it has aged, but that's part of its charm, right? This house has seen us through happy, care-free times as well as troubled and worried times. The house seems to hold emotions, good and bad, just a like a good friend who holds your secrets and nevertheless loves you and accepts you as you are.

Eventually, we had to sell the house, which was hard. But, looking back, I realize that we don't need the house to keep its happy memories. Besides, it's busy helping a new family make their own memories.

MEMORIES OF GRANDPARENTS

To pass on the knowledge of a unique individual rather than just an image in a portrait is a true gift. Not everyone has had the privilege of knowing any, much less all, of their grandparents. Even fewer have memories of their great-grandparents. That's part of what makes our memories of grandparents such treasures.

Because the relationships we had (or lacked) with these elders often molded us, at least in part, into the individuals we are, these memories are important to note and preserve. In addition, future generations that won't have the privilege of knowing these relatives will appreciate an insight into their personalities and lives. Regardless of how large a part your grandparents played in your upbringing, great conversations can result when you share your memories of your grandparents with younger family members.

When others read our stories and memories of our grandparents, they come to understand us better. As readers gain a richer understanding of these people who influenced our lives, by extension they acquire insight into how our personalities and family traditions developed.

Writing about grandparents also allows readers a glimpse of your family history. We recently experienced this firsthand while exploring old photos and records with my husband's parents. I had often heard that my father-in-law's Grandmother DeBarr was eccentric. Looking through old photos, my mother-in-law remembered her first meeting with the woman. After a few minutes with the intended bride, Grandma DeBarr looked at her grandson and announced in a disgruntled tone, "She seems all right for a dark-headed woman."

Apparently, in his Grandma DeBarr's view, fair-headed women were less likely to be evil than dark-headed ones. Although I knew much about this woman from family history research, that small anecdote gave me a much deeper insight into her than the photos and genealogical information.

Now when I run across her photo, I ponder at her countenance and wonder what it would have been like to have known her.

My grandmother's Treasure Chest had many such grandparent gems. One detail that I loved reading was how one relative wore his hat everywhere but to church, and how, on Sunday mornings, her eyes were always drawn to the white "blaze" on his forehead. Her comparison of his untanned forehead to a horse's marking endeared them both to me. Similarly, I love remembering the grin my own grandpa wore every time he called his black dog, which he had saddled with the unlikely moniker *Snowball*.

Don't leave out small details or think of them as insignificant. Small traits, such as a farmer's tan, crooked smile, or favorite joke, can help your readers better picture the people about whom you write. Many times, those little memories are just the things that strike a chord with your readers. Try describing your grandparents. When you look at their photographs, what do you remember? What do you know about them? What did they look like? What were they like? What types of things were they apt to do or say?

If you only knew your grandparents as a child or didn't know your grandparents at all, you can still write the stories you've heard over the years. Ask other family members—it will be worth finding out.

Additional Tools:

Worksheet: Memories of my Grandparent guides you as you develop ideas for writing about your grandparent or grandparents.

My Turn: My Grandpa Wilkinson relates some memories of my paternal grandfather.

Worksheet: Memories of my Grandparent

Use this worksheet to jot down what you know and remember about your grandparent. (Feel free to make a copy for each grandparent.)

Grandparent's Name (paternal/maternal):_____

Today's date:_____

The Genealogical Facts: (Include any facts you know: full name, place of birth, date of birth, date of marriage, date of death, place of death, where they lived, military service, and so on.)

Where your grandparent lived and how far that was from the place you grew up:

Physical description of your grandparent and details that stand out in your memory: (hairstyle or lack thereof, clothing, mannerisms, and so forth)

Words you'd use to describe your grandparent's personality: (happy-go-lucky, serious, intense, irascible, free-living, religious, devout, giggly, nurturing, and so on)

Compare your grandparent to a well-known book or TV character: (For example, "like Aunt Bee with a husband minus the southern drawl.")

Describe how close you were to your grandparents:

Things you remember doing with your grandparent:

Hobbies or vacations you shared with your grandparents:

Jot down notes for any other thoughts or attributes about your grandparent that could be worked into stories here: (family lore, career or occupation, military or church service, and so on)

My Turn: My Grandpa Wilkinson

Sadly, I don't have many vivid memories of my paternal grandfather, Harvey L. Wilkinson. He was hospitalized with emphysema when I was only five and died when I was seven.

What memories I do have are more like impressions: him in the background of the room, keeping things calm and smiling kindly. One of the few clear memories I have is of sitting on the arm of his burgundy reclining chair in his living room. He would read me the funnies out of the newspaper. If my attention wandered from the comics, it would be to stare at the deep, crisscrossing lines on his dark bronze neck.

My sister and I with our grandpa.

Isn't it strange that I remember the back of his neck better than his face?

My imagination and my parents' stories about him served to fill in the blanks of my memory. I remember taking great pride in the fact that my grandpa was a WWI hero, based on seeing his picture in the Danville, Virginia, newspaper. Forty years later, doing genealogical research, I discovered his military records.

At the time of his draft registration, he was living in Detroit, Michigan, working for the Hathway Motor Company as a machinist. Because of his knowledge of automobiles, my grandfather was made a wagoner in the army, which entailed taking care of the vehicles assigned to his unit. Ironically, he was assigned to a unit without automotive vehicles, so during the war, he served in Europe as a private caring for the horses assigned to his unit. This was probably the best possible job for a kind-hearted man who wanted to serve his country in such a terrible war.

That newspaper article? Grandpa had been chosen commander of his local veterans' group.

That doesn't make him any less of a hero to me.

Newspaper article about my grandfather, complete with his name misspelled.

FAMILY LORE

Oral Traditions

Every family has stories that have been passed down for generations. We're all familiar with them. We know them by heart whether or not we were there when they happened. They are the stories that have been told, often with embellishment, about our family members since our youth.

You might already know all the details of these stories by heart, or you may need to do further research. If your recall is fuzzy, don't hesitate to go to other sources to fill in missing details. You can contact your relatives and ask them what they remember.

Stories of family lore will vary. Some are pivotal, crucial chapters in your family's history, while others are small anecdotes or comical victories of everyday life. Some stories will be lighthearted; others will be grave. Whether it is a story of your ancestors moving across a continent or outsmarting of a fox trying to get to the hens, record these long-told stories. Regardless of their import, these stories have a place in your Treasure Chest.

Accuracy may not be possible. Likewise, it may not be possible to confirm the event itself, but your role here is not that of a journalist. Your role is to convey the essence of a fine family tradition of storytelling. For genealogical purposes, though, please *do* note if the story is unconfirmed. It might even be fun to note the different versions of the story. You could tell the story as your parents told it, then note the differences in the way your uncle told it. If you have been able to do any research to determine the accuracy of the tale, note that as well.

Pay special attention to those stories that shaped your family history. Rags-to-riches stories, military heroism, and outstanding athleticism can form family traditions. Even small family stories about this can be interesting. For instance, my grandmother's family resided in Lunenburg County, Virginia, for generations, and my grandmother dreamed of one day going to New York City. Though she never did, my mom and dad honeymooned there (on my mother's first trip outside of the state). When I studied abroad, my grandmother was thrilled for me. Her unfulfilled dreams of travel helped both my mom and me to make sure our dreams came true. They may have also caused us to savor our good fortune—and our wanderlust—all the more.

Take some time and think back about the stories and traditions that run in your family. Use the included brainstorming worksheets to help you. Go ahead and preserve a piece of family lore.

Additional Tools:

Worksheet: Brainstorming for Stories of Family Lore sparks recall about the stories in your family.

My Turn: When Daddy was a Little Girl describes a humorous family story.

Worksheet: Brainstorming about Family Lore

Use these sheets to tickle your memory and jot down ideas about things you might want to write about. Remember, no full sentences! This is just a bank for your ideas.

Stories about the "old country" or the "home place":

Stories (not personal memories) that you remember about your ancestors:

Skeletons in the family closet:

Cultural or ethnic heritage of your family:

Important traditions in your family:

Professions and work ethics of your ancestors and grandparents:

Common names or birthdates in your family:

Family members named after ancestors:

War stories or stories of life in the "olden days":

Stories behind old pictures or old portraits that have hung on the wall for generations:

Stories of immigration and migration—why ancestors settled where they settled:

My Turn: When Daddy Was a Little Girl

It's not unusual for a little girl to hear her mother begin a story with, "Back when I was a little girl . . ." It is unusual when the speaker is the little girl's father.

No, this isn't a transgender story.

Fun with Daddy.

My dad loved to kid kids. Sometimes he loved it more than my mom thought wise. He honed his craft on his own children. For instance, he used to tell us that spinach was grass that a cow had already eaten once. Not to side too much with my mom, but I didn't start eating spinach until I was over thirty.

At my grandparents' house, a framed picture of my dad as a toddler hung in the hallway. In it, he was wearing what appeared to be a dress. Most fathers would have explained that the "dress" was a gown that was traditional for babies in the early 1930s. Instead, he contended that he was not always a male—when he was young, he was a little girl.

My sister and I were gullible but not that gullible. The fact that we never believed him, however, didn't dissuade him from insisting. Perhaps it was his way of fitting into an all-female household—he could always claim he could relate based on his past as a little girl.

What's more likely, though, is that he just liked to stir things up.

When my daddy was a little girl.

FAMILY HEIRLOOMS

Heirlooms aren't just objects with significant cash value. In fact, the objects we treasure often have less monetary value than emotional significance. Regardless of the dollar value of an object, succeeding generations will be able to more deeply appreciate an object if they know its heritage. Indeed, once an object's story is known, its status will greatly increase among its keepers. It makes sense to leave a record of the object's story in your Treasure Chest so that family members can more deeply appreciate its emotional value.

It's always interesting to see an object mentioned in a written family history. It's almost as if owning an object passed on by ancestor gives the possessor a more tangible connection to that relative. A case in point comes from my grandmother's Treasure Chest. After my parents' sudden deaths, my sister and I had a terrible time sorting through all the things in their house and deciding which ones had value as we determined the disposition of their belongings. I chose to keep a dark mantle clock that's not in the best condition and no longer keeps time based only on a vague memory of it being in my grandparents' house and the fact that it appealed to me. Later, I was quite pleased to find while reading my grandmother's Treasure Chest that my grandmother remembered that clock from her youth on her grandfather's farm. She used to find comfort in its tick-tock response to the problems she confided to it. She also wrote that years later the clock seemed to "hurry the time along" on special occasions. Her memories of the clock make it that much more precious to me. It definitely qualifies as an heirloom in my book.

Heirlooms can be a bit like flowers. One person's flowers are another person's weeds. So how do you figure what you want to pull and what you want to fertilize? Anything that your relative or ancestor cherished enough to keep or hand down over the years might hold enough emotional value to qualify as a family heirloom. On the other hand, the fact that these items are still around might simply be indicative of someone's inability to part with things. Asking questions about items is the best way to separate the kitsch from the valuables and find items that might lead to a story.

Simply examining an object often gives you a closer connection to its owners. Even if the relatives aren't around or up to interviews, with a little research, you might find some great stories. The worksheet at the end of this section will guide you.

Don't limit yourself to objects in your possession. Perhaps these heirlooms take permanent residence with a sibling or an in-law. Regardless, their history, insofar as it relates to your family's history, is worth documenting.

It's entirely up to you whether you want to assess the monetary value of your heirlooms. If you're interested in insuring your heirlooms, divvying items up fairly, or investing money in preserving them, bringing in an expert appraiser can be very helpful. However, you don't need a dollar amount to know the value on an heirloom in your heart.

Additional Tools:

Worksheet: Identifying Family Heirlooms helps you find objects with stories in your family.

My Turn: The Little Table tells the history of a treasured piece of furniture.

Worksheet: Identifying Family Heirlooms

This worksheet requires more looking around and asking questions than writing down ideas—though you might want to jot down notes as you go. Explore the toolshed, garage, attic, or barn. Ask relatives about the objects you find, their origins, and their stories. Even if they've only been kept around for their aesthetic or financial value, it might be interesting to know what other homes they've graced and if they were purchased (or, better yet, made) for some special occasion. Even if you don't find an heirloom, you may get an education. As you explore, keep a special eye out for the following:

Are there objects that you have had in your home all your life?

Look around as if you're a visitor. What looks old or unique? What doesn't quite fit in with the rest of the decor?

Do you have any boxes that have been lurking in the basement or the back of a closet for decades? Pull them out and start investigating.

Ask about objects that are in relatives' homes as well, including any old boxes that might be lurking about. There could be treasures in those such as wedding invitations, graduation programs, funeral programs, and more. Ask about old Bibles, prayer books, and military and professional awards.

Travel Treasures

Ask about any objects brought back from military or business travel overseas. See if you can find out when and for whom they were purchased. Why was the purchaser traveling? Many stories accompany travelers' keepsakes, and one story can easily lead to another.

Furniture and Bedding

Is there any handmade furniture in the family? Look for markings on furniture that will identify its maker and when it was made. Ask relatives about its origins.

Don't forget textiles—especially quilts. These are often handed down from generation to generation.

Look at old photographs and pay special attention to the backgrounds. Do you recognize any of the objects in the pictures?

Decorations and Religious Articles

Holiday decorations and religious articles often have stories behind them as well. Where were they made? Who were the original owners? Look for things like prayer shawls, menorahs, nativity sets, or prayer rugs.

Family Bibles are a particular gem because they were sometimes the main repository for family birth, death, and marriage records.

Tools of the Trade

Military artifacts—uniforms, helmets, or medals can give clues to ancestors' military service, rank, deployment, and time of discharge.

Professional tools or equipment, such as an old sewing machine from a seamstress or tailor, furniture from a carpenter, and so on, might reveal what a family member's life was like in times past. Exploring the tools and asking questions about them will certainly lead to stories of one sort or another.

Personal or hobby mementos such as artwork, travel souvenirs, handmade gifts, or items purchased far away can reveal information about travels, income, and personal taste. Old postcards and letters often prove to be a veritable fountain of information. Of course, the fact that the relic was relegated to the attic or garage might be part of the story as well.

Research

Research the trade tools you find. Once you know how the tool related to a profession, you can better judge if it's a treasured keepsake or a piece of clutter.

Collectibles such as blown glass, figurines, dolls, stamps, coins, and favorite toys, and items made in occupied Japan often have both financial and emotional value.

Look at old family wills. If your family doesn't have possession of them, talk to a research librarian about how to find copies. Wills enumerate possessions that were valued at the time. With a description of objects that were passed down, it's easier to figure out if those objects are still in the family—and maybe even in your house.

My Turn: The Little Table

The little table

When my husband's grandparents moved from Pittsburgh to Grand Rapids, I finally got a chance to know my grandfather-in-law better. He was particularly tickled that my husband, the only remaining male Hedgecock in his line, had married. He had great hopes for more male Hedgecocks. One of the things he loved to talk about was a little wooden table. He would brag that it had been in Hedgecock hands for generations.

Recently, I found more information about that little drop leaf table. Richard Adams Falkinham, whose daughter married into the Hedgecock line, made it. Richard left Boston, where he was working as a cabinet-maker, in 1842 and moved to Burnett, Wisconsin, where he was one of the original settlers. There his cabinetry skills were put to the uncomfortable but practical use of making coffins for those who did not survive the bitter Wisconsin winters.

The little table is not only a nice piece of craftsmanship but also a piece of history in a family of pioneers. It will always be treasured.

RICHARD ADAMS FALKINHAM IS DEAD

Patriarch of the Town of Burnett and probably the Oldest Pioneer
Settler of Dodge County, is Called Away Monday
Afternoon, May 3, at 3:30 o'clock at
the Age of 96 Years.

Headlines in the 1904 Horicon (Wisconsin) Reporter

FAMILY TRADITIONS AND RECIPES

It's great to pass on family traditions even if you don't know their origins. If you do know, even better! The more deeply succeeding generations understand the meaning behind traditions, the more the practices will resonate with them later in life. It will also serve to connect them with their elders; following in the footsteps of mothers and grandmothers (or fathers and grandfathers) imbues a deeper meaning to practices and rituals.

Food Traditions

It's not surprising that family recipes are treasured. Food is often an integral part of our traditions, and some dishes carry rich traditions themselves. The smells and tastes of these familiar treats evoke the past. Suddenly you'll be back in your grandma's kitchen, waiting for the pie to cool enough to cut. Even the ingredients of recipes reveal much about the culture from which they originated. In addition, ethnic and religious traditions are deeply entwined with recipes and the way food is prepared.

Practicing food preparation traditions can be a sensory-rich experience. Memories associated with smells, tastes, and sounds surface quickly when triggered. Though neither of my grandmothers lived close to us while we were growing up, I have very distinct memories of their kitchens and some of the dishes they liked to cook. To this day, eating or smelling similar dishes can take me back to the days when my feet still swung above the floor and I sat at their tables. Author Staci Troilo remembers the importance of food in her Italian family's kitchen:

> Tables will be laden with steaming soups, sautéed vegetables, trays of antipasti, and dozens of cookies and cakes. The most amazing part is that the meals are prepared by memory, the recipes passed down not on stained cards but at the elbows of mothers and grandmothers in crowded kitchens. And we wouldn't have it any other way.[1]

Even recipes for less important events can become family traditions. For instance, although my mother-in-law's baked bean recipe is not a secret, she's the one who makes it. We could try to replicate it, but eating her baked beans is part of the fun of a family get-together. Similarly, my mom passed on a passion for highly personalized birthday cakes. I remember a particularly inspired Cinderella cake—a Bundt cake with orange icing and a banana stem iced green. As a matter of tradition, my sons' birthday cakes have ranged from space shuttles to dragons.

Other Traditions

Often, when we think of preserving traditions, we forget about the little things that define the rhythms of our family's dynamics. Describe the routines around your house that have become precious rituals, whether they involve kids or not. Include such things as inside jokes, funny sayings, favorite stories, and Sunday afternoon activities in your Treasure Chest.

Writing about traditions and recipes is not the only way to keep them alive. We (and our children, cousins, spouses, nieces, and nephews) learn by doing. The absolute best way to preserve traditions is to spend time practicing and teaching these traditions to your family members. They might start out as rituals, but over time, they can become vehicles for your family members to connect with their past, their family's heritage, and people they love and remember.

Go ahead and write about the traditions—both big and small—that characterize your family.

Additional Tools:

Worksheet: Brainstorming for Family Traditions and Recipes guides you as you brainstorm about traditions both big and small.

My Turn: Frozen Treat for the Frozen tells of the tradition behind a favorite treat.

1. Staci Troilo, "Recipe for Prosperity," Guest post at TreasureChestofMemories.com (blog), March 20, 2013, http://treasurechestofmemories.com/recipe-for-posterity.

Worksheet: Brainstorming for Family Traditions and Recipes

Use these sheets to tickle your memory and jot down ideas about things you might want to write about. Remember, no full sentences! This is just a bank for your ideas.

Big Traditions

What traditions spring from your ethnic heritage? (such as tartans for those of Scottish descent)

What traditions spring from your religious heritage? (for example, baptisms, first communions, namings, and traditions centered around Christmas Eve, Easter Sunday, Rosh Hashanah, Yom Kippur, or Ramadan)

What traditions have been passed on from your family's vocational heritage? (For example, farming families might take part in 4-H fairs; fire fighters' families might attend local parades.)

What weekly traditions kept time at your home? (such as meatloaf on Tuesdays, bathroom and housecleaning on Saturdays, or visiting Grandma on Sundays)

Were any hobbies passed on from generation to generation? How did these hobbies help you bond?

Recipes

Look at your responses to the questions above. Do any of these traditions have a food component?

Does your family prepare certain meals for special occasions? (for instance, collard greens and black-eyed peas on New Year's Day or a standard Saturday morning breakfast)

Are there any meals that only Grandma (or someone else) could make?

Is there any food that was normal for your family but not quite mainstream in the rest of your community? (such as drinking coke with salted peanuts in it or having waffles for dinner)

Little Traditions

Does your family have any bedtime stories or routines?

Did your family often go to the same place on vacations? What drew you there? What did you do there?

Does your family have any service traditions? Did you traditionally pitch in at local Habitat for Humanity builds, go on mission trips, or do fundraiser walks? Why did that particular charity resonate with you or other family members?

What little sayings were repeated over the years? Did some become inside jokes?

Sometimes describing a typical day will help you home in on the little traditions. Try writing about a typical day as a child, spouse, young parent, and so on.

My Turn: Frozen Treats for the Frozen

A little knowledge can ruin all your fun.

Back in the days before we knew about pollution and acid rain, a South Carolina snowfall would spell more than hours of sledding. When we finally did plod home on frozen feet, we'd be given hot chocolate and "snow cream."

My guess is that my hometown of Spartanburg owned a snowplow in the '60s, but I doubt it owned many. Snowfalls did not last long, but when they came, it was an enforced holiday. No one went anywhere. (It's not only my family that had the tradition of running to the store for bread and milk as soon as snow of any amount was forecast. So many Spartanburgers did this that stores would run out. No hint of a lie—there would be a single inch of snow on the ground and the 7-Eleven's shelves would be bare.) Snow days were a party!

According to my sister, our recipe for snow cream is:

1 big bowl of snow (Our mom always used her full-size mixing bowl)
1 cup milk, half-and-half, cream, or any combination thereof—whatever you happen to have (Remember the part about South Carolinians and their wont to buy milk at the first sign of any impending snowstorm? We always had milk.)
1/4 cup sugar
1 tsp. vanilla
My personal memory has a pinch of salt and at least one egg involved, but that was before we knew about salmonella.
Mix milk (or substitute), sugar, and vanilla until the sugar dissolves. Then pour it over the snow and stir. Voila, snow cream! Enjoy in front of the fire.

Despite the fact that I have lived twenty years in Michigan, where snowfalls are common and hated, that little-girl "IT'S GONNA SNOW!!!" excitement still fills me whenever it snows. With warm memories of friends, fireplaces, hot chocolate, and snow cream, I feel joy watching the barren landscape assume its fragile mantle of white.

ANIMAL STORIES

If you're an animal lover, you understand what an important role these creatures can play in our lives. But you don't have to be completely gaga about animals for them to take their rightful place in your Treasure Chest. Whether it was a pet lending comfort and unconditional love, a farm animal that your family depended on for its livelihood, or a wild animal that kept you vexed and entertained, it's likely that an animal played a starring role in some memorable moments of your past.

Family Pets

Pets and companion animals add comfort, unconditional love, dirt, goofiness, dander, and more than a little comedy to their households.

My dad and his friend

Compared to the rough roads and ups and downs often encountered with our human family and friends, our relationships with our pets are incredibly simple. Imagine going to the friendship pound and picking out a new human friend. "Let's see, that one's kind of cute and didn't immediately bite my face off. I bet that if I am decent to him, he'll be a loyal companion to me the rest of his life." Even when pets aren't as loyal as their billing, their motives are transparent, and understanding those motives tempers any hurt. For instance, if I'm eating a salad and my husband is eating a steak, you can guess which one of us the dog loves best. I understand why my dog is directing a worshipful countenance towards my husband, and I know that the worship will be over with my husband's last bite. The dog's loyalty to me will then be restored, at least until someone offers to take him on a walk.

When you write about pets, you won't just preserve your memories; your writing will entertain your readers and reveal your affection for your furry companion—and showcase your sense of humor. (It might also reveal why your veterinarian's kids were able to have such extensive orthodontia, but let's not dwell on that.)

Other Animals

It's not just companion animals that rate a mention in your Treasure Chest. Observing wild animals can be fascinating. Furthermore, some of the favorite stories in my family are stories of attempting to outwit some animal or attempting to live peacefully alongside other creatures. The fact that an encounter with an animal made for a memorable moment is telling. Whether or not your loved ones share the same level of infatuation with animals, they will appreciate what it meant to you.

Coming from a long line of animal lovers, I have greatly enjoyed my grandmother's descriptions of the animals around their farm and stories of the animals in their house. I especially treasure her writings about being cheered by the site of a beautiful bird or alarmed at the sight of a fox. If your family shares this affection for furry and feathered (or even scaled) friends, add these stories to your Treasure Chest.

Additional Tools:

Worksheet: Brainstorming for Animal Stories will tickle your recall to help you collect memories of animals in your past.

My Turn: Paper Route Pogo relates a story of a spaniel with his own paper route.

Worksheet: Brainstorming about Animal Stories

Use this worksheet to tickle your memory and jot down ideas about the animals you might want to write about. As always, remember: you don't need to use full sentences. This is just a bank for your ideas.

Write down the names of any pets or wild animal rescues you have had. Include their breed, if applicable, known, or knowable.

Is there a story behind their name?

Think back. Did you acquire them in any interesting way? Were any of them strays or rescues?

Are there any special relationships between the animals sharing your home or property (such as battles between dogs and ground hogs or bonding between cats and dogs)?

Did your pet(s) have any of the following adventures, mishaps, or encounters?

Stealing food from the table or counter:

Getting into the trash:

Fighting with other dogs or cats:

Run-ins with wild animals:

Adventures with human hunters:

Chasing cars:

Chasing or herding kids:

Jumping fences:

Encounters with the UPS guy, the postman, or the paperboy:

Getting lost:

Getting stinky:

Bath time adventures:

Invading a party:

Embarrassing behavior with visitors:

Pet sitting adventures:

Miscellaneous

Did your pet distinguish his- or herself with agility?

Did your pet distinguish his- or herself with barking or meowing volume?

Did you pet have other vocalization talents?

Did your pet have any other unusual habits or proclivities?

Did your pet have an unusual nemesis?

Did your pet have other unusual characteristics?

Was there ever a time that one or more of these pets were a particular comfort to have around?

My Turn: Paper Route Pogo

My husband has something in common with the springer spaniel I had in my youth: they both had a paper route.

Whereas my husband's paper route was the result of his entrepreneurial spirit, the dog's was based on his unique relationship with our neighbors. Well, that and a love of treats.

This was in the late seventies on a dead-end street where leash laws, if existent, weren't enforced. Pogo Beauregard Wilkinson, an English springer spaniel, romped through the neighborhood and exerted his ownership over the entire lower third, not just our house. Unless, of course, someone acted as though they were going to challenge him. Pogo was a lover, not a fighter, and would run away whimpering if anyone took an aggressive step towards him.

Pogo, as he neared "retirement" age

Pogo had some strong springer instincts that he adapted to his advantage. He loved pointing and would point at every bird. He would also point when a car drove up, but not at the car. He was just showing off, knowing that his full tail and featherings looked particularly beautiful in a point.

Pogo also loved carrying things. Having been adopted by a non-hunting family, he satisfied this craving for years with his daily duty of carrying in the junk mail, which evolved into carrying the newspaper.

We had a long driveway, and the delivery boy for the *Spartanburg Herald Journal* would always toss the newspaper at the bottom of it. Somehow Pogo figured out (as far as we know, no one purposely taught him), that if he ran out in advance of the newspaper fetcher (usually my father) and brought the paper in, he'd get a treat. Soon he'd respond to "Get the paper, Pogo" and would dash out and bring in the paper. Pogo got a little bigheaded about his success. He teased my dad on cold days, refusing to get the paper until Daddy went about twenty yards down the driveway. This dog wasn't bearing the cold alone.

Since his paper-fetching-for-a-treat venture was working so well for him at home, he decided to expand. Each morning after he retrieved our paper, he'd run out and wait for a neighbor to come out to get theirs. Gradually, one by one, he trained three or four other neighbors to wait for him to bring them their papers. He'd come to their doors, paper in mouth, and be richly rewarded with praise and treats.

He continued his route as I went off to college but at some point went into voluntary retirement. He was probably the best, and without question the best looking, delivery boy the *Spartanburg Herald Journal* ever had.

LESSONS LEARNED

Just as we are keepers of memories, we are keepers of lessons learned. The kindly thing to do with the wisdom we've gained is to share it with those we love and with generations to come. We've all suffered our lumps and bumps on our life journeys, and if we're lucky, we've learned a few lessons from the jolts. If we're luckier still, we will have learned a thing or two by observing others.

There's an old story about why a dog doesn't live as long as a human does. This folk wisdom, inevitably attributed to a child, explains that dogs don't have to live as long to learn their life lessons because they already know how to love, play, and be loyal. Humans, in comparison, take longer to learn those things, and thus need to live much longer. Although this fable is less than flattering to humans, the flip side of being such slow learners is that we have many more stories about those life lessons than dogs do.

That isn't to say that others can simply read about our experiences and avoid their own lessons. But we do learn from one another's stories, especially stories that are similar to our own. As you write about the times that you were schooled in life, your loved ones will more deeply relate to you, whether they are relating to you because they recognize part of their own lives in your memories or because they are learning something new about you. This will often give your readers more than just insight into how you became the person you are—it might also give them a good laugh.

Lessons Learned Report

If you come from the business world, you might be familiar with a Lesson Learned Report. These reports tend to start with lessons gleaned from simple, operationally defined problems, concluding with the advantages of the lesson learned or that outcomes to avoid in the future. If you're familiar with this format and like it, you can adapt it for your Treasure Chest. A touch of irony or sarcasm can prevent your writing from sounding dry. For example:

"Keep small children in your sight at all times, even when you're cleaning up messes they've made. Children placed in one room while their babysitter cleans up a mess in another room have often been found to engage in further undesirable behavior, such as stripping naked, covering themselves with stickers, and downing an entire bottle of Hershey's chocolate syrup. Such escalations of naughtiness can cause an exponential increase in messiness—such as the puking of said syrup or the stickers stopping up the bathtub drain."

Sometimes very succinct summaries of comedic lessons can also work well: "John quickly learned that Mom freaks out when he uses the square stickers with the US flag on them to decorate his bicycle."

Both the above methods break the "show, don't tell" rule that writing coaches like writers to follow. However, they are in keeping with another common rule of good writing, which goes something like, "As soon as you learn the rules, get creative and break them." Sometimes leaving things to the imagination is okay.

Tell Your Stories

You can also simply tell the story of what happened. If you'd like to present the lesson learned in a comedic light, it's good to leave a surprise for the reader at the end. Tell of the day the kids made a huge mess and you cleaned it up, only to find that meanwhile, your little one was covering himself with stickers and making himself a chocolate milkshake without the milk, ice cream, or shaking.

If the lesson you learned is not at all funny, or you'd prefer to present it in a more serious light, simply write from the heart. Share what you've learned and why it matters. Your loved ones will appreciate your openness and honesty. The worksheet that follows will help you discern which lessons you'd like to leave a written record about.

Additional Tools:

Worksheet: Brainstorming Lessons Learned helps you identify the events and stories behind the lessons you've learned.

My Turn: BFFs explains how the author learned what a BFF was way before the term (or the Internet) was invented.

Worksheet: Brainstorming Lessons Learned

As you read the prompts below, think carefully about which life situations taught you important lessons. Make enough notes that you can come back and develop stories out of the ones that resonate most with you.

How I learned the value of hard work:

How I learned to be prepared:

How I learned there was more to life than material things:

How I learned to stop and smell the roses:

How I learned that it is more (or just as) blessed to give as to receive:

How I learned to love someone else more than myself:

How I learned to be careful what I prayed for:

How I learned to love my neighbor:

How I learned to love the unlovely, mean, or sick:

How I learned how to put on a happy face:

How I learned the meaning of loss:

How I learned that I was blessed:

How I learned to persevere:

How I learned to pick my battles:

How I learned to say no:

How I learned to walk away:

How I learned not to respond to every taunt:

How I learned not to sweat the small stuff:

How I learned that things often happen for a reason:

How I learned the value of community:

How I learned to love myself:

How I learned to trust myself:

How I learned to trust God:

How I learned the power of prayer:

How I learned to trust my instincts:

How I learned to stand up for myself:

How I learned who my real friends were:

How I learned to rise to the occasion:

How I learned not to wear my emotions on my sleeve:

How I learned patience:

How I learned tact:

How I learned to rely on the kindness of others, at least occasionally:

How I learned to appreciate random acts of kindness:

How I learned to pay it forward:

How I learned to mind my manners:

How I learned the meaning of hospitality:

How I learned to hold my head up:

How I learned to be the advocate:

How I learned what was most important or what mattered most to me:

My Turn: BFFs

In the early seventies, we didn't say BFF, but we knew what it was. Learning what that meant under less than ideal circumstances was one of my most memorable lessons.

Sally Moore and I grew up during the times when kids were allowed to spend the summer entertaining themselves. We roamed around the neighborhood, climbed trees, created waterfalls and swimming holes in the creek, played hide-and-seek in the fields, and rotated from house to house to play. We would lunch at whatever house we happened to find ourselves at mealtime. Most times, it was the Moore's, not because Sally was diabetic and had special menus, but because Sally's dad was the assistant manager of Sears, which meant that Sally had the coolest Barbie accessories. We all knew to be back at our own homes by six or our moms would "call" us. By call, I mean bellow so loud that everyone within a mile radius knew who was late for dinner.

We weren't allowed to do all this barefoot, though we usually did. One day, while crossing the field behind my house, Sally stepped on a thorn. We weren't supposed to be in the field, and we weren't supposed to be barefoot. I thought the simplest solution would be the take the thorn out, go home, and wash Sally's foot. Sally, howling in pain, refused to consider that. She also refused to let me go get help. Normally easygoing, Sally became obstinate. When I asked to see the thorn, she started threatening me through her tears. She told me that if I touched the thorn, our friendship would be over. She said she would never, ever speak to me again.

I started to cry too.

There we sat in the field, crying—Sally over the pain in her foot; me at the dilemma of Sally either being really mad at me (or worse) or continuing to watch Sally cry over her foot. The field was sweltering hot, and we were nowhere close to any shade from the South Carolina afternoon sun. Eventually, despite my better judgment, I reached over and plucked the thorn out of her foot, then closed my eyes and cringed, waiting for the onslaught of Sally's anger.

What I got instead was a huge hug and Sally saying, "You're the best friend anyone could ever have!" I sat there in amazement. When I asked her why she wasn't mad, she explained it to me as though it were as clear as the nose on my face. "You did what I needed even when I told you not to!"

Sally moved to Wilmington, North Carolina, the next year. We eventually lost touch, but I've never lost touch with the lesson she taught me that hot afternoon with blood, sweat, and tears.

Sally, if you're out there, I still think of you as my first BFF.

SCHOOL DAYS

The image of a tongue stuck to a frozen flagpole is familiar to all of us. Even if we never did that, we (or our siblings or cousins) had some equally half-baked escapades. Such high jinks are almost rituals of childhood, and such memories, established during our formative years, remain particularly poignant. They continue to resonate in our old age. They have an effect not only on us but on all those who shared these experiences or who were involved in similar antics.

Memories of a common basic human experience inevitably strike a chord with us because they ring so true to our own memories. Most of us have vivid memories of going to school. Despite the intervening decades, they remain crystal clear to us. The universal commonality of school memories, however, can give the writer pause. There's no question that we have a lot of material. The question becomes, how do we make such a common experience fresh and interesting?

Although school days are a common backdrop for all of us, the details can be quite different. The urban school experiences are often quite different from rural ones. Schools and school experiences will differ based on economics, time period, location, and region. Whether it's a general description of your school or the story of a specific moment, highlight these salient points so that your readers know to what degree your school days sync with theirs.

Tell stories, not just facts. Most readers won't find a recitation of teacher and school names interesting. Rather, they want to know about the experiences that stand out most vividly in your memories, whether they are funny, sad, typical, or unique. Your readers will also be interested in a general description of your school days, especially if they were different from those of today or those of your other family members.

Think of stories you would reminisce about at a school reunion. Those are the stories that are apt to write themselves to some degree. Go into enough detail that your readers can get a feel for what school was like at that time, in that place, and under those circumstances. When your memory does stumble upon some facts like names or dates, explain how those facts were significant to you. You can also explain how they played a role in the stories you write.

Develop the characters of your past. If your memory revolves around a teacher, don't simply list that teacher's name and physical description. Describe such things as voice, habits, and approachability. For example, the simple description of a short sixth-grade teacher with frosted hair gives readers a vague mental image of a character of your past. She is, however, less interesting than Mrs. V., who was not only known for her frequent use of a particularly shrill police whistle to establish peace but also for making kids who tried to cheat their way into the Clean Your Plate list drink their milk, complete with the peas and whatever else they had stuffed into the carton.

Many memories of our school days are fragmented. For these memories, an episodic approach makes a lot of sense. Many people enjoy listing random memories of their schools. Episodes don't have to be dramatic or traumatic to be worth a mention. For instance, I remember reading under my desk through much of the fifth grade. That might not be a story, but it is telling. I might also mention that I was marked as "inattentive" on every single report card throughout my elementary school career. Such details help your readers connect to you.

Some of us sailed through our school days with only the rare dramatic episode. As you relate your school memories, be sure to point out your role in your class or peer group. Were you an instigator, a follower, a teacher's pet, or an observer giggling behind the hand that hid your smile? If you were a participant, write about it! If you were strongly influenced by something you observed, write about that too.

Your Turn

To get your ideas percolating, look back at any old photo albums, scrapbooks, yearbooks, or boxes of mementos. The two supplemental worksheets will help you come up with themes and topics about which to write. One last thing: don't forget the three-miles-in–a-blizzard-uphill-with-no-shoes part.

Additional Tools

Worksheet: Idea Bank for School Memories will help you recall a wealth of details and school memories to write about.

Worksheet: School Days Memories in a Word sparks creativity as it challenges you to look back on your school days from a fresh perspective.

My Turn: The Test I Missed is the story of a quintessential playground confrontation.

Worksheet: Idea Bank for School Memories

*Build yourself an idea bank of school memories. Whenever a prompt reso-
nates with you, jot down your notes. If your experiences were unusual (at least
by today's standards), mark them with an asterisk. You'll want to expand upon
these points.*

Your School

What was the name of your school? What years did you attend? Where
was your school located?

How many grades were in the school?

What were your best and worst subjects?

How many students attended your school? In high school, how many
students were in your graduating class?

What did kids wear to your school? (such as styles, uniforms, and fads)

Did you participate in sports or other extra-curricular activities?

Did you have any favorite after-school hangouts?

What was your first-ever day of school like? (Describe the teacher, your
friends, and special happenings. Surely I wasn't the ONLY one to
be paddled on my first day of school!)

Did you have any annual first-day-of-school routines? (meeting the
teacher, receiving teacher assignments, finding out who was in
class with you, taking siblings to school, what you dreaded, what
you looked forward to, new clothes, and so on)

Did you teachers have any amusing foibles? What things did they do
that wouldn't be allowed today?

How did teachers help, inspire, or become role models to you?

Who was your favorite teacher and why?

Did you ever have a crush on a teacher?

Did you ever dream of being just like a teacher?

What was the principal like? Should that word really end in *pal*?

What school policies were there for tardies, lunchtime, recess, games, Valentine's Day, or other events?

Did you walk or ride to school? Were there any noteworthy experiences on the way? Did you always get there?

Were you ever—or often—the new kid?

Did you have to deal with bullies?

Did you have any memorable illnesses, actual or feigned?

Did you have any playground incidents or injuries?

The School Building

How big was your school building?

What did it look like? (such as brick, sprawling, new, old, with or without air-conditioning)

Did you ever go back as an adult? Is it still a school?

Do you still live nearby? What do you remember most as you drive by?

Are there any smells or sounds you remember?

Classmates

Which classmates stand out in your memory? Why?

Were any notorious? For what were they notorious?

Did your class have the complete complement of pretty, gawky, dumb, bookworm, jock, kind, mean, and weird kids? Which stand out in your memory? How did they differ from the assortments at any other schools?

Did you attend all K–12 grades with the same group of classmates, or did you meet many of them somewhere along the way?

How did one or more of your classmates influence your eventual life choices?

Did any one person (guest, staff, or classmate) inspire you?

What kind of student were you?

What kinds of assessments did your school give?

Did you have any significant learning disabilities?

Was prom a bid deal or no deal?

Did you win any awards from the school or student body? Include anything from perfect attendance to "Most Likely to be Incarcerated."

Were there any other important components, like cars, emergencies, romance, or rivalries with other kids or schools?

On a scale of 1–10, with ten being happy and one being miserable, how happy were your school days? Why?

Superlatives and Extremes

What was your absolute best moment of school?

When were you the most embarrassed?

What made you the happiest?

What hurt you the most?

What was your dumbest decision or klutziest move?

What was the greatest wisdom you learned or saw in school?

Looking back, what experiences did you have in school that you see mirrored in your children or other loved ones?

Most Likely

If a "most likely to" vote were held in your elementary school, what would the vote have been for you?

If a "most likely to" vote were held in your middle or junior high school, what would the vote have been for you?

If a "most likely to" vote was held high school, what did you win? If not, what should you have won?

Were the votes right? Why or why not?

Has all this remembering brought any more thoughts to the forefront? Jot down your notes!

Worksheet: School Days in a Word

As you write about your school memories, you will want to characterize your younger self for your readers. Using just one word, describe yourself during the following phases of school:

1st day of school

Kindergarten

4th grade

Middle School or Junior High

High school freshman

High school senior

High school graduate

Describe yourself as you think others saw you during your senior year of high school as a:

Song title (Song doesn't have to be popular—you can make one up if you want.)

Flower

Car

Beverage

Book title

My Turn: The Test I Missed

Note: The names of the children have been changed.

The front playground at Woodland Heights Elementary School looked idyllic in the late '60s. In fact, it still does. The baseball diamond was next to an oak tree near the road, and there was other play equipment and acres of green grass on which to hang out. But, like many playgrounds, it wasn't idyllic for everyone. To some kids, it seemed like a torture ground. Some of us coped by avoidance. When I was forced to wear corrective shoes for my flat feet, I would simply come down with a terrible stomachache right before recess each day. I preferred to spend my recesses with my head down on my desk rather than facing the teasing. Even after my mom and doctor decided my self-esteem was suffering more than my feet ever would and tossed the clunky, ugly (and expensive) shoes, for me, the playground was never the place of safe haven and happiness it was designed to be. It was the place of being picked last for kickball and having friends turn on you.

I learned to tread carefully there.

Not everyone else did.

My friend Jane, a sweet, pretty, popular girl with hair the color of spun gold, was always at home here. Of course, she was never the last one to be picked. Another friend, Mary, a tall girl with long straight hair, refused to let the playground cow her. Much less popular than Jane, and possibly even less popular than me, Mary was true to her own self. She wouldn't join cliques or bow to peer pressure. She walked about self-assuredly, not caring who judged her.

These two girls were perhaps destined to collide. I was home sick the day they did and never fully understood the details of what transpired, but Mary and Jane had a confrontation. It was decided that the conflict could be resolved by a simple popularity vote. Those who took Jane's side would form a circle around Jane. Those who took Mary's side would form a circle around Mary. By the time the vote was over, everyone on the playground, save one, had gone to Jane's circle. Only one friend, a tiny dark-headed girl named Carolyn, who was almost painfully shy, stood by Mary.

I missed the test, but Carolyn aced it. Like me, Carolyn also liked Jane. She was not confrontational, yet she scored high marks on courage, personal integrity, loyalty, and fairness. In my mind's eye, I can still see her small frame standing alone next to her tall friend, facing the rest of the sixth grade girls. I continue to admire her to this day.

I often wonder why it was that I was destined to miss the test that day. I wonder if I would have scored as well as Carolyn.

It was quite the wake-up call for me. It taught me that you have to stay ready. You never know when life is going to throw a pop quiz at you.

EVERYDAY QUESTIONS

Soul Searching & Wondering

A Treasure Chest is not just filled with lessons learned. Questions belong here too. We certainly don't want to leave behind the impression that we've figured it all out! All of us have things we perpetually puzzle over. We seethe over injustices and betrayals and wonder how people can treat each other so poorly. Other times we look at our world and wonder if peace on Earth will ever be possible, or even if peace at home is possible. We wonder if there is hope for the future.

Our wonderings aren't always about issues on the magnitude of world hunger or universal peace. We also have times in which we think about life's little questions: what the right thing to do is, how to raise children, the evolutionary value of zits, or how to stop procrastinating. We may have moments in which we contemplate the vastness of the universe or the beauty of a flower.

Writing about these questions is truly a page from my grandmother's book—one from which we all get tremendous enjoyment. Sometimes, instead of reflecting on her memories or relating historical stories, she simply put forth a question that was gnawing at her brain at that time. Through her writing, she would chew on the issue a bit and then (at the risk of taking the metaphor too far) leave it for us to digest or not. Most of the time, she wouldn't solve her mental dilemma through her writing. Instead, she left it open so that her readers could gain insight or, occasionally, humor from it.

That's not to say that you can't include the pondering of imponderables. You can and you should. The things over which we ruminate are revealing. They not only give a glimpse of the person behind the thoughts, but they also put those thoughts into context. The type of thing that occupies your thoughts doesn't just divulge your values; it tells much about the society you live in, the company you keep, the events in your life, and your connections to those things. If you write openly, you can put these things into the context of your hopes and dreams.

A Treasure Chest represents the things that have mattered and continue to matter to you, making unexpected treasures out of those questions that always seem to pop up on the horizon or trip you up when you're not expecting them. Include them. Whether it's a heartfelt lament over why bad things happen to good people or wondering if the kids really think you're so dumb that you don't know folded clothes in the clothes hamper probably aren't dirty, give your loved ones a glimpse into the things that keep you awake at night, stick in your craw, and remain in your prayers.

Additional Tools:

Worksheet: Idea Bank for Everyday Questions helps you develop a bounty of topics to write about in your Treasure Chest.

My Turn: Does God Have Three Feet, and Why Can't He Keep His Shoes Tied? uses a humorous tone to delve into a serious dilemma.

Worksheet: Idea Bank for Everyday Questions

Look at the following list of ideas of things about which people might wonder. Mark any that resonate with you and jot down your ideas.

Questions about Faith

Is there a God?

Is there a heaven? If so, what is heaven like?

If heaven is perfect, are there golf courses for golfers, bowling alleys for bowlers, and so on?

Do animals, particularly pets, go to heaven?

Who created God?

What things do you want to ask God when you get up there? (for example, why good people suffer, why there's so much pain in the world, why are we made as we are, or why it's so hard to get answers sometimes)

How does God answer prayer?

How do we know what we "just know"? What is a conscience?

How to know when to compassionately keep my mouth shut versus speaking out for what's right?

Are there miracles? If so, why don't they always happen?

Why didn't God make us (or our brains) with an off switch?

Questions about Life

Evolution, creation, or both?

What's the purpose of life? What's the purpose of your life?

How do you make life matter?

How do you stop procrastinating?

Why do you love others?

Why do others love you?

Why are (or aren't) you good for another person?

What things do you wonder about late at night? What things keep you from falling asleep?

Introspective Questions

Is your glass half-full or half-empty?

Is it better to be trustful and risk being hurt or distrustful and risk closing yourself off from others?

When others disappoint you, what do you wish they had done differently? Why did they behave the way they did?

What principles do you have that others don't share? Why or why not?

Why are you happy in your lifestyle? Why might a loved one not find happiness in this lifestyle?

Nursing a grudge? Tired of nursing a grudge? What would it take to let go? What would it take to forgive?

Why do we lash out at people we love?

Why does forgiveness matter?

If you could start over, what would you would be when you grew up?

What was your dream for your life? Why? Are you living it?

What happens if you don't know what to dream for?

Are you supposed to be trying to change the world?

If you were face death tomorrow, what would your biggest regret be?

Are you doing what you are meant to do?

Can one person make a difference?

Why do we care what other people think?

Is it important that other people like you or think you're attractive? Why?

What would my ancestors think of me and my lifestyle?

Questions that Arise During Times of Stress or Crisis

Why are some people so mean?

Why didn't you see _____ coming?

At your worst moments, from whom did you draw companionship? From whom or what did you draw strength?

Is it better to see someone you love waste away slowly or die suddenly?

Where does politically correct end and disingenuous begin?

Child Rearing Questions

How do you teach kids to be happy?

How do you teach kids to have faith?

How do you teach kids to be honest?

How do you teach kids to do the right thing?

How do you teach kids to have courage?

How do you teach kids to value the things you value?

How do you teach kids to be humble yet have good self-esteem?

How do you teach kids to avoid the mistakes you've made?

How do you get siblings to stop arguing with each other? Is such arguing natural? Is it in any way helpful?

How much should you nag kids about their grades?

Should all kids play sports?

Is it getting easier or harder to raise children? Was it easier when you were a child?

How do you let your child be independent?

If raising a teen, do you mistrust your teenager? Do you mistrust the job you did raising your teenager?

Smaller Questions

Why does toast always land butter-side down?

Why do cats gravitate toward the one person in the room who doesn't like cats?

Can you ever start a sentence with "I don't mean to be rude" or "no offense" without being rude or offensive in the rest of the sentence?

Why do we spend so much on pets and give so little to the poor?

What else do you wonder about? Use a blank page to jot down your questions—big and small.

My Turn: Does God Have Three Feet, and Why Can't He Keep His Shoes Tied?

A few years ago, I was looking for a book titled something like *How to Keep your Faith and Teach it to your Children* when I found Rabbi Marc Gellman's *"Always Wear Clean Underwear!" and Other Ways Parents Say "I love you."* In this wonderful book, short, humorous essays for kids explain what parents are really saying when they say things like "walk the dog" and "always wear clean underwear." However, it's not only the kids that we speak to in such vague terms. Here's what I mean when I say, "Lord, please keep your shoes tied."

My personal theology doesn't include a God that sits around causing calamity or inflicting torment on everyday innocent people that he has mistaken for Job. Neither do I think God is so hapless that he can't keep track of his shoes. Nevertheless, the metaphor of waiting for the other shoe to drop does resonate with me.

Regardless of what my faith and intellect tell me, when I'm clipping around feeling like I have life by the tail and then get dumped on by a big, fat, hairy, ugly, life-changing disaster, it does feel exactly like some type of celestial shoe (or combat boot) has fallen from the upper exosphere to flatten me. There are times I find myself going through life with an uneasy eye on the future—and poised to duck. I'm perpetually waiting for the other shoe to drop, though perhaps unjustifiably so. Based on the number of shoes already cast in my direction, I should feel safe. Forgive my abuse of the metaphor, but based on my personal experience, I'm starting to wonder how many shoes God wears.

My intellect, my faith, and my less neurotic side want to reject the idea of heavenly shoe dropping. Not only do I not think that God punishes, I firmly believe God is omniscient enough to keep his shoes tied if he were to wear any. Tragedies are not heaven-sent, and our faith in God is what can see us through tragedies when they do occur. What I need to do is trust more and worry less. That would put the matter to rest for me if it weren't for my kids.

When it comes to my children, I struggle to trust God with their welfare. I do trust God in a long-term way to see them through life, guide them in becoming what my aunt would call "fine young men," and endowing their lives with meaning and happiness. That trust clashes markedly, however, with my God-given maternal instinct to protect them from all hurt and harm.

Perhaps that's the reason why, as I converse with the Divine, I occasionally beg, "Lord, please keep your shoes tied."

RECALLING THE MORE ELUSIVE CHILDHOOD MEMORIES

Putting childhood memories into categories such as school days, friends, or animal stories does more than lend organization to your writing. You are also putting your stories into context, which is the way our brains store and retrieve memories that make sense in a given situation.[1] For instance, because a word has more meaning to most of us than a string of numbers, we can remember a telephone number that is spelled out for us much more easily than we can remember the numeric version.[2]

This is what's happening when we use worksheets or prompts to boost our memories. The greater context you have in which to frame your memory, the easier recall becomes. If someone asked me to remember playing outside as a kid, my memories might include some biking. But if I were asked, more precisely, to remember the first time I rode a bike without training wheels, I would remember the color of my bike (dark blue), the wind in my face and hair, and the sudden realization that my dad's 225-pound footfalls were far behind me. I can still remember the exhilaration of doing it by myself mixed with anger with my dad for letting go. I can also remember that anger evaporating when I realized that his ear-to-ear grin wasn't so much a pleased-as-punch-with-himself smile as it was a smile of pride for my accomplishment.

Unfortunately, not all memories come floating so easily to the surface, and not all can be so easily set into context. Often, they surprise us when they do surface. When we unexpectedly remember an event, person, smell, or feeling, the immediate reaction is often, "I had almost forgotten!" But is that true? Did we almost forget, or did we just fail to retrieve the memory until that very moment?

As the aged and those suffering from degenerative neurological disorders have taught us, early childhood memories remain clear and available to us even when we are unable to retrieve memories of the recent past. However, every memory of our childhood does not stay with us. My sister remembers events in our shared past that are completely missing in my memory bank and vice versa. What makes some memories stay with us so long while others fade away? What makes the recall of some memories so elusive? Part of the answer lies in understanding context and meaningfulness.

Emotional Meaningfulness

There's no denying that some of our most vivid memories are those with a strong emotional significance. We remember our wedding day or taking our kids to the emergency room. When events take place in the midst of emotional circumstances, our memories of them often remain vivid—even when we don't want them to. This emotional significance is why so many of us can remember the first time we met our spouse-to-be or where we were when the twin towers were attacked in New York City. Likewise, adults of my parents' generation remember unequivocally where they were, whom they were with, and what they were doing when they heard about the attack on Pearl Harbor.

Some events may not have seemed emotional at the time, but they may have a secondary emotional significance because they played a part in who we became. When I flew to Europe to study, my flight was one of the last to leave its Atlanta concourse. As the plane began to taxi, I caught a glimpse of my father standing at the end of the empty concourse, watching our departure. At the time, I was struck by how small and vulnerable my very large father looked in that moment. And, although it caused a catch in my throat and my twenty-year-old self's sense of independence, I didn't realize that I'd recall that moment often later in life.

Scientists confirm that emotional meaningfulness is key in storing memories because it is related to the release of norepinephrine, a brain chemical similar to adrenaline.[3] This means that memories of events that took place during emotional circumstances are stored more efficiently. Those moments that my sister and I shared that only she remembers invariably had a greater emotional significance to her than to me. Not surprisingly, she doesn't remember the day that some of the neighborhood girls challenged the best of the tree-climbing boys to out-climb Laura. I do. Why? Because I won, and that mattered to me.

Often, when emotions are triggered, memories of times we felt a similar way come rushing back to us. We might remember nothing about besting a bully until we find our child in a situation with a bully. Some people, for instance, have deeply repressed memories of violence that erupt years later when they are again confronted with a violent or dangerous situation. Seeing a grandchild for the first time can likewise bring memories of new parenthood rushing back to us. This also explains the reemergence of my airport memory of my father. When we look back at our childhoods with an eye toward moments that were significant to us, emotionally or otherwise, we can often revive these elusive memories.

Sensory Context

It's not only emotional memories that can be elicited by surprise. Another context of memories is physical sensation. Often, a sensory experience—such as a sound, texture, or smell—triggers almost-forgotten recollections. Think of sitting by a bonfire on a summer night, complete with the heat on your face, the smell of smoke, and the sound of logs crackling. Memories float to the surface on wings of scent, sound, and touch. In *A Natural History of the Senses*, Diane Ackerman gives a particularly eloquent explanation of the relationship between our olfactory facilities and recall:

> Nothing is more memorable than a smell. One scent can be unexpected, momentary, and fleeting, yet conjure up a childhood summer beside a lake in the Poconos, . . . another, hours of passion on a moonlit beach . . . a third, a family dinner of pot roast, noodle pudding, and sweet potatoes, during a myrtle-mad August in a midwestern town, when both of one's parents were alive. Smells detonate softly in our memory like poignant land mines, hidden under the weedy mass of many years and experiences. Hit a tripwire of smell, and memories explode all at once. A complex vision leaps out of the undergrowth.[4]

Those trying to recall a circumstance are often more successful when they intentionally surround themselves with similar sensations. A sound, smell, or feeling can take us back decades, bringing our childhood memories to the forefront of our minds.

This works particularly well with less-common sensory stimuli. Think of where your mind goes when you get a whiff of cotton candy, taste licorice, or hear someone opening a can of tennis balls. Even common sensations, such as feeling the hot sun on our backs, smelling a sea-salt breeze, or hearing a bird's evening song, are also capable of coaxing memories to the surface. When our contact with these sensations is unplanned, the memory tends to surprise us. Think when you've felt moved to say, "Ah, this brings back memories." Chances

Sun, sand, and surf still remind me of family.

are, there was a sensory impetus to that comment—like warming yourself in front of a wood stove, sampling an old-fashioned cookie, roasting marshmallows, or enjoying the total immersion sensory experience of sledding down a hill.

If you have the luxury of re-creating the sensory environment—like revisiting a farm or baking a loved one's favorite recipe—engage your senses and tap into those hidden memories.

Your Turn

We've already put many memories into context or categories. Now we'll try to brainstorm for more—the almost-forgotten memories. Use the two worksheets to brainstorm and recollect your childhood memories.

Additional Tools:

Worksheet: Brainstorming Other Childhood Memories will spark your recall with lists of common childhood situations that have potential for emotional significance.

Worksheet: Idea Bank for Sensory Triggers helps you brainstorm for memories against the backdrop of sensory experiences.

My Turn: Not-So-Lazy Summer Days describes the sensory-rich fun of summer days.

1. Tony W. Buchanan, "Retrieval of Emotional Memories," National Institutes of Health Public Access, (2008), accessed March 13, 2014, http://www.ncbi.nlm.nih.gov/pmc/articles/PMC2265099/.

2. Joshua Foer, *Moonwalking With Einstein* (London, Penguin, 2011), 164.

3. Keith Tully and Vadim Y Bolshakov, "Emotional Enhancement of Memory: How Norepinephrine Enables Synaptic Plasticity," *Molecular Brain*, (2010), accessed February 17, 2014, http://www.molecularbrain.com/content/pdf/1756-6606-3-15.pdf.

4. Diane Ackerman, *A Natural History of the Senses* (New York: Vintage Books, 1990), 5.

Worksheet: Brainstorming Other Childhood Memories

Look at the following list of ideas. If any strike a chord, jot down some notes. As you do, include notes about context, both emotional and sensory, so that you can come back to them later to develop a story.

Telling ghost stories:

Vacations or camping trips:

Family Reunions:

Weird relatives:

Childhood pranks:

Getting busted: (by parents, teachers, or law enforcement)

First jobs: paper routes, babysitting, and so forth

Fairs:

Bonfires or campfires:

Backyard games:

Scars and how you got them:

Church:

Youth Group Trips: (church, school, music, and so on)

Nature: (time enjoying it as well as disasters)

Food:

Dreams:

Clothes:

Sports, music lessons, dance recitals, and other extra-curricular activities:

First kiss:

Worksheet: Idea Bank for Sensory Triggers

Under each heading, write down what smells, tastes, sounds, and tactile sensations evoke memories for you. Also note what memories or stories come to mind.

Tastes: (lemonade, gingersnaps, cotton candy, Thanksgiving dinner, and so on)

Smells: (like locker rooms, cookies in the oven, pipe smoke, grandma's perfume, new car leather, or incense in church)

Sounds: (such as bike horns, fireworks, snapping beans, tap shoes, the crack of a baseball bat, a soccer ball being kicked, a dog's tail thumping, and foreign languages being spoken)

Tactile Sensations: (like the slimy bottom of a creek, hot sand on a beach, jumping in ice-cold water, frozen feet on snowy day, your pet's fur, going barefoot in grass or on hot asphalt, and playing your favorite sport)

My Turn: Not-So-Lazy Summer Days

Summer days were idyllic for the little girls on the street where I grew up. Not idyllic in the fairy princess sense, but idyllic in the civil engineering sense.

Right across the street from our house was an empty lot that connected to undeveloped wooded acreage behind our subdivision. Through the woods ran a creek with runoff from a man-made lake. Although there were a lot of days that we played inside each other's houses, much more time was spent outside—climbing trees when we were supervised and building forts, bridges, and dams when we weren't. The creek took a bend right at a clearing in the woods. We'd play until we were hot and miserable, then "swim" in the waters that pooled at the bend. "Swimming" in the creek was a little less restrictive than "swimming" in your average bathtub, but not by much. However, on hot South Carolina days, it was just the thing to cool you off after strenuous tree climbing, tag, or whatever other games we'd come up with.

Looking back, I have particularly fond memories of the summer we went up the creek to a place where the elevation changed. Working all summer, we greatly enhanced the beauty (at least in our opinion) and flow of the creek by creating a series of waterfalls. The mud would squish between our toes (no shoes for this gang), the sun would burn hot on our skin, and our muscles would burn with exertion, but all that would be cooled by the water. By summer's end, there was a much bigger swimming hole at the base of the falls. We'd stretch out in the pool and revel in the waters falling over our heads. Sitting in our pool and feeling the force of the water on our heads and backs was singularly invigorating. We had conspired with nature to create a slice of paradise.

Though we were seldom out of the yelling range of our parents, the woods gave us an illusion of privacy and freedom. Sometimes I wonder if we missed out by not going to summer camps and taking part in organized sports. Even if we did, I don't mind. I wouldn't trade those summer days for anything.

MATERIAL SOLICITED
FROM RELATIVES

You don't have to be on a quest to memorialize an entire family's history to find it useful to gather tidbits and stories from relatives. If, like me, you no longer have access to your parents' memories, relatives can be virtual fonts of inspiration and information. (They often have great photos, too.)

Who in your family most likes to tell stories about the olden days? Conversely, who in your family do you know the least about? Who in your family seems to be the repository for family Bibles, photo albums, portraits, and heirlooms? Next time you're visiting, you might just want to pull out one of these items and start asking that person questions.

Chances are they won't be reluctant to share. Older people often relish going through old photos and memorabilia and reminiscing about times gone by. They particularly relish fresh ears eager to hear their stories. Part of the joy of this type of memory collecting is simply spending time with your loved ones. Be sure you're not so goal oriented that you forget to enjoy your visit.

You can also plan interviews with relatives. In these instances, it pays to organize before you go. Particularly if you have a concrete goal for the interview, write down what you want to ask in advance. You can direct your interview by the way you frame your questions. Think carefully about how you want to structure them, considering your goals as well as your interviewee's personality. Think about how loquacious your relative is as well as how quickly he or she will tire. Ideally, your interview should allow the interviewee to indulge in some tangents, but ensure that you can get them back to critical topics.

Consider the following examples of questions an interviewer might ask her grandmother and the structure she might use to pose them.

Yes-No questions

Yes-no questions, like any questions that limit responses to a couple of options, aren't the best way to encourage a subject to talk freely. They work best for situations in which you want to limit the scope of the interviewee's answer.[1] Although effective in pinning down a politician's position on an issue, yes-no questions can be intimidating to relatives. When you want an expansive answer, framing questions in this manner can be counterproductive. For example, responses to "Do you remember when you met Grandpa for the first time?" could include "Yes!" followed by a pregnant pause.

On the other hand, if you're interviewing a relative that tires easily, yes-no questions such as "Did you marry Grandpa at the First Baptist church?" allow them to quickly confirm information.

Open-ended questions

Open-ended questions don't make any assumptions about the intended answer or seek to influence its flow. Although journalists argue that open-ended questions can allow a source to duck an issue or to ramble, they often work well for family storywriters.

Journalism expert Lou Granato points out, "Asking open-ended questions encourages a source to open up topic areas that you might not have considered."[2] Use your judgment on when to use open-ended questions in your interview session. A question such as "What do you remember about the first time you met grandpa?" could elicit various responses—including long-winded ones. If you are going to interview talkative family members, and if you have scheduled plenty of time and have backup batteries for your recorder, such open-ended questions might serve your purposes well. Relax and enjoy your time with a person that matters to you. If you need to keep you interviewee on-topic, there's another option.

Leading questions

Journalists avoid leading questions because they can influence a responder's answer.[3] However, these questions often work well for family memory collectors. Remember, we're not wearing a journalist's hat in most interviews with relatives. It's perfectly acceptable for us to have an agenda. If your grandparents have been married for sixty years and are not constantly at each other's throats, chances are they have a beautiful love story to share. You might want to facilitate your grandmother's storytelling by asking a leading question. If you ask, "Tell me about how you met and fell in love with Grandpa," you are likely to get a love story in response.

When there is a particular story or truth you want to preserve, it's fine to lead your loved ones a little to get them headed down memory lane. In fact, all questions are valid as long as you are both enjoying the stroll.

Interview

You know what information is missing from your family history and what information would be most meaningful to you and your loved ones. In informal settings, simply sitting down with someone and conversing will provide great stories. Going through old photographs (don't ignore the scribbles on the backs), scrapbooks, family Bibles, and other documents with a relative will often yield a bounty of information without any need for a formal or planned interview. If you do want to ask questions, start with open-ended ones, letting your interviewee lead you along their own path. My perennial favorite is to ask how couples met. A worksheet with a list of possible questions that you can use is included at the end of this section. (For in-depth sources and ideas, see the Recommended Resources section.)

As you listen to your relatives' accounts of their pasts, note their use of language and try to preserve any unique or uncommon phrases or word usages. (There will be more to follow on this topic in Language: Gatekeeper of Place and Time.) Also, to whatever extent possible, cite what you know—such as who originally passed the story down, when it happened, and the full names of those involved.

Handy Tools

Recorders: The aforementioned handy little voice recorder will aid your memory as you transcribe your notes—as well as prevent note-taking from interfering with the flow of information. Depending on the quality of the recording and the clarity of your interviewee's voice, you can even use voice recognition software to transcribe. Digital recorders offer another advantage: later, if you use a blog or website format, you can insert the sound file and let the person featured tell part of the story in his or her own words and voice.

Fill-in books: Especially if you're far away, the many beautiful books meant for eliciting the memories from relatives can be immensely helpful. You can find them in bookstores or order them from Internet booksellers.

It's easy to find one suited to the person or persons you have in mind and give it to them as a gift. The gift will be returned to you (and your children) many times over.

Additional tools:

Worksheet: Questions for Relatives helps you decide which questions to ask in interviews with loved ones.

My Turn: ID-ed illustrates how looking through photographs with relatives can yield a surprising story.

1. Len Granato, *Newspaper Feature Writing*, (Australia, University of New South Wales Press, 2003), 24.

2. Ibid.

3. Gordana Igric, "Tips for successful investigative journalism," Media Helping Media, August 6,2012, http://www.mediahelpingmedia.org/training-resources/investiga-tive-journalism/583-successful-investigative-journalism.

Worksheet: Questions for Relatives

Your interview, as well as the questions you ask, will vary greatly depending on the relationship you have with your interviewee. Here are some sample questions you might want to include. As you go through the list, note the relatives you'd like to pose each question to.

What was your mother like?

What was your father like?

What language was spoken in your childhood home?

How far away from other relatives did you live?

While growing up, did you ever get in serious trouble with your parents?

Were there any times when your siblings got in trouble?

Were you particularly close to any of your siblings growing up?

Did you have pets or animals growing up?

Where did you go to school?

Were you brought up in a church, mosque, or synagogue? Which one?

When did you have your first job? What did you do?

Did you have any adventures before you met your spouse?

Are you a veteran? Which wars? What experiences did you have?

How did you meet your spouse?

What was your courtship like?

Do you remember when you first met your future in-laws? What was that like?

What was your wedding like? Did the whole family come?

Where did you live when you were first married?

When did you start your profession?

Were your children born at home or at a hospital?

What was it like when your children were born?

Have you lived in any interesting places?

Were there difficult times that you had to get through? How did you cope?

Did you live through wartime? What do you think now when you reflect back on those times?

Did you live through any times of political upheaval? What do you think now when you reflect back on those times?

Did you experience any historical moments, like the JFK assassination? What are your memories about those times?

What do you think has been your greatest accomplishment?

What do you think has brought you the most happiness and contentment in life?

What advice would you give to a young couple starting their lives together?

What advice would you give to a young person just beginning college?

Do you think you were lucky to grow up in the time and place that you did?

My Turn: ID-ed

Having relatives point themselves out in old photographs can yield more information than you'd expect. At least, that's been my experience.

Once, while my aunt Cathy and uncle Joe were visiting, I pulled out my box of miscellaneous photos and souvenirs that I'd inherited from my parents, hoping they could give me insight into some of the items. What I got was insight into growing up dirt poor on a Virginia farm during the Great Depression.

We came across an eight-by-ten photograph of the tiny Pleasant Grove School from 1937 with kids of all ages posed in front of it. I wasn't sure

Pleasant Grove School 1937

if my mom, who would have been about six years old at the time, was in the photo. Looking at it, Uncle Joe told me that my mom wasn't in the group, but he was. With what I like to call the "professor twinkle" in his eye, he asked my aunt to find him in the photo. Sure he'd come across a way to stump her, he waited with a hint of a smirk on his face. It transformed into an expression of astonishment as my aunt quickly and confidently pointed to a boy in the front row.

"How'd you do that so fast?" my uncle demanded.

"Simple," replied my aunt, who clearly enjoyed schooling the professor. "There's only one boy with no shoes."

Uncle Joe is second from the left.

SHARE WITH ME MY SORROW AND I'LL SHARE WITH YOU MY JOY

Those who love us do so in good times and bad. They may love to laugh with us, but because they care about us, they are also interested in and touched by memories and reflections of times that weren't so rosy. While you don't want to leave a whine fest as a legacy, don't hold back your memories of darker days for fear of burdening someone.

Writing about those times can be therapeutic for you and others. Grief and hurt sometimes have to be expressed. This is especially true when you strive to gain and share understanding through your writing. You can explain or state what happened and how you felt without indulging in accusations, name-calling, or self-pity. Your readers will understand from your tone that it is not a plea for sympathy but rather an account of a less happy time. Your purpose may be reflecting on what you learned from your darker days and how you got beyond it, or it might simply be the contemplation of how a loss is going to affect you.

While I can't say that I enjoy reading my grandmother's account of the day my grandfather died, I *am* touched by it. I am moved not just by the rawness of her grief and the magnitude of her loss but also by the depth of the love in which my roots are planted. I am even more deeply touched that she chose to memorialize and share her feelings. To me, though it's difficult to read, it is a treasure.

Sometimes it's not just life that's imperfect. Sometimes we are. Writing that draws from common human experience captivates readers. Emotional vulnerability is just such an experience. Every reader has had their bad times, and unless they are very young, every reader has certainly experienced losses in life as well. Just as we find it easier to get close to someone who acknowledges their imperfections, it's easier to connect to a writer who has known some moments of vulnerability. In *Courage and Craft: Writing Your Life into Story*, Barbara Abercrombie expounds, "No one wants to read about your perfect life unless you walked over burning coals to get there. Humor yes, perfection no."[1]

There's another reason to include the sorrows—they provide an emotional backdrop for many of the memories and reflections that follow. Our losses have shaped us. We can't hope or expect our loved ones to fully understand the form our lives have taken if we hide the very events that did the forming and shaping. In short, you have to know of the dark to understand and appreciate the light. The rays of hope that come out of our troubled times will not shine for others without a view of the storms that preceded them.

Even if we agree that we want to include a record of the bumps in the road that we have encountered on our life's journey, we can still pick and choose which ones we want to write about. Some of our bad times were simply unpleasant times that we had to fumble our way through. Other times, we come out the other side of an experience a changed person.

How do you determine which events were simply sad or difficult times that you just got through as opposed to events that truly shaped you? Identify a time in your life that was difficult. Write honestly about it. After you've gotten some of your thoughts and emotions on paper, you can consider taking the additional step of sharing it. You can even have a version that you keep to yourself and an edited version that you share with others.

Additional Tools:

Writing Exercise: My Life as a River helps you contemplate memories of darker times that you might want to include in your Treasure Chest.

My Turn: Like the Columns of Old Main shows how friendship pulled me through some very difficult hours

1. Barbara Abercrombie, *Courage and Craft: Writing Your Life into Story* (Novato, CA: New World Library, 2007), 58.

Writing Exercise: "My Life as a River"

Tools: Paper, pencil, and eraser.

Instructions: Give yourself twenty or thirty minutes. Imagine your life as a river. Drawing with a pencil, begin charting the course that your river has taken. As you think about the following points, adjust the course of your river as necessary. Feel free to erase and redraw as you reconsider. When you river changes course, consider whether it was a gentle change or an abrupt U-turn. Don't forget to include the markers (like boulders and submerged rocks) that caused the water to become tumultuous or calm. Draw or label them, whether they're internal (such as faith, maturity, or personal growth) or external (such as job changes, life changes, loss, or romance). You can even include weather, which can be whatever metaphor you like for contributing factors such as health, wealth, or the people around you.

Which times in your life have you experienced calm waters?

What was happening in your life at those times?

Mark the internal and external influences that caused the current to calm.

Were you able to relax and bask in the calm, or did you grow restless?

Was your river running straight? Meandering? Branching out?

When did the current move quickly?

What increased the flow?

Was there white water? (Draw it in if you're so inclined.)

Was it a joyful ride, or did you feel like you were going under? (Label this.)

What events and influences were affecting the current at these times?

Did you feel like you had the safety of an inflated tube, or did you wish for a helmet?

Did you feel like you had an oar or a paddle to navigate or influence the ride, or were you tossed about with no means of controlling events?

Did the white water grow into rapids? Were they dangerous? Were there submerged rocks or whirlpools that seemed inescapable?

Was there a dangerous waterfall? How close did you come to going over? What stopped or saved you—or did you go over?

Was there beauty in the danger?

Did the water ever become stagnant? Why?

What changes did you yearn for at these times?

What did you do about it? What happened?

How do you feel about your river's course? What insight have you gained?

How do you see your river continuing into the future?

My Turn: Like the Columns of Old Main

It's difficult to explain my memory of the days immediately following my parents' deaths in a car accident. Some moments are like an old filmstrip haphazardly spliced together. Other moments are preserved in replayable high-definition 3-D, as fresh as if they occurred yesterday. In these memories, I can feel the air temperature and the rawness in my throat. I can hear my own voice.

Within twenty-four hours of getting the news, we returned to Spartanburg, South Carolina, where my parents had lived and where I had attended Wofford College. In fact, the funeral home was just down the street from the Wofford campus. I remember passing the campus, yearning for the innocence of my time there but feeling that it was forbidden territory. I could almost see Old Main, the historic building at the figurative and geographic center of the campus. My innocence had already been stripped away when a drunk driver had killed my dear friend Laura two years earlier. Now I was about to bury both of my parents. I averted my face from the campus as we drove by. Returning to those happy-go-lucky days was inconceivable.

The visitation at the funeral home was overwhelming. Friends of my parents filed in by the hundreds. I felt as if I were floating away, losing contact with reality—an observer in someone else's bad dream. Many of these people's kind words and grief are lost in the bad splicing of my memory, but one moment in particular stands out. In fact, tears of gratitude still well in my eyes when I think back on it. Someone tapped me on the shoulder and pointed in the adjacent room. There, saddled together on a couch, were three of my suitemates from Wofford College. They had traveled from Mississippi, North Carolina, and nearby Greenville. After quick hugs, they told me they would be there for me throughout the evening and the funeral the following day. True to their word, and although I was busy with other visitors, they were close by, watching me—willing me to be all right.

Their presence supported me as steadfastly as the columns of Old Main brace the building's timeless façade. It was not their sympathy that moved me; it was their support. The love of these friends, Helen, Janet, and Ann-Marie, was a palpable force keeping me upright, enabling me to greet my parents' friends and help them through their grief.

Since that day in the funeral home, the image of Old Main has not only embodied classical architecture and an institution of higher learning but also a place where I found lifelong friends—and my roots. Fifteen years later, a beautiful print of Old Main graces my hallway. It doesn't show the columns, but, like my friends who live far away, I know they are there, providing support through the years.

CONVERSATIONS
FROM THE PAST

Sometimes, it's not just the story we want to convey but also the companionship itself—the interpersonal dynamics we shared with or observed between loved ones. The conversations we shared and the banter we enjoyed demonstrate the various facets of relationships. Such exchanges reveal the ease of friendship or kinship; shared history and humor; and the personalities and propensities of the people involved.

It's great to tell about banter and conversations, but telling doesn't always capture their essence. So how do we capture those long-ago conversations? By going back to one of the foundations of writing: show, don't tell.

The obvious way to connect to conversations from your past is re-creating, to the best of your ability, a typical or memorable conversation. Perhaps it was the first time you received insight into a relative or just a funny line that a kid said. Alternatively, you might want to preserve a conversation that was a pivotal point in your relationship. It's great if you can still remember the blow-by-blow account. If not, don't despair. You don't have to recount the entire conversation as an unabbreviated or verbatim dialogue; most of the time, a concise description of the situation and what transpired ending with a simple quote or two will get the message across just fine while still keeping your readers engaged.

In these circumstances, accuracy becomes a gray area. An accurate re-creation does not necessarily mean getting each word right. It means getting the gist of the conversation, *as you remember it*, right. In fact, it may be more helpful to reframe the concept of accuracy as *truth*. In our family, we have a story about my mom that revolves around her trying to open what I remember to be a milk carton. My mom used to claim that we got it wrong because it was an orange juice carton that she was opening. If I'm retelling the story, the carton will remain a milk carton because (a) that's the way *I* remember it, and (b) the type of carton doesn't impact the essence, or emotional truth, of the story. The emotional truth of the matter is that my mother, feeling cranky and stubborn, as a matter of principle struggled to open the more difficult side of the beverage carton (despite helpful advise from her husband, daughters, and the carton itself) because no *#$% carton was going dictate where she had to open it.

Like this story, many of these conversations are the ones we enjoy telling at family reunions and get-togethers. Re-creating these conversations in print keeps them from getting lost to future generations. Just recently, a ninety-year-old friend told me about her first date with her husband. She took a lot of glee in telling me that when her then-suitor showed up at a church dinner, her long-time friend couldn't resist admonishing him, "You better be somebody special if you're here looking for Mary!" I dearly hope that my friend has preserved, in writing, this memory for her kids! It reveals a lot about Mary that her friends were screening her callers.

As you relate these conversations, be sure to let your characters' (yours and your loved ones') individuality shine through. Think about those interactions that have been flavored with brutal honesty or brightened by humorous subtext and revive those exchanges.

There is, of course, a more introspective way to handle this. Sometimes fate and circumstances prevent us from having the conversations we'd like to have or wish we'd had with people that matter (or mattered) to us. You *can*, however, re-create a conversation that you wish you'd had with someone. It might be more difficult because you are predicting the behavior and speech of other people from your knowledge of them rather than simply reporting events as they occurred. What were their strongest values and traits? How would they react or express themselves? The onus is on you to be fair and accurate.

Many of us will be surprised at how easily this comes. I certainly was when I tried this method. Luckily, the common experiences and values of our past are deeply ingrained in us. We know with relative certainty how a friend or family member would react and often even know what they would have said. The truly difficult (yet rewarding) part is addressing the conversations that you wish you'd and revealing a more vulnerable side of your nature.

Regardless of how you do it, re-creating conversations not only allows others a glimpse into your past but allows them to see how you became the person you are.

Additional Tools:

Worksheet: Brainstorming Conversations helps you identify which past conversations you want to record.

Worksheet: Capturing Past Conversations guides you as you re-create a conversation you remember.

Worksheet: Conversations You Wish You Had guides you as you write about a conversation you wish you had.

My Turn: Conversation in the Car relates a short but hilarious conversation verbatim.

Worksheet: Brainstorming Conversations

The following is a list of ideas of conversation topics. Circle the ones about which you feel you could write. Make notes about the situation and who was involved. If a topic is more applicable to a conversation you wish had taken place, note that as well. As always, add your own ideas as you go.

- Self-discipline

- Self-esteem (or lack thereof)

- Healing emotional wounds

- Dealing with chronic disease or pain

- Advocating for children

- Achieving/teaching life balance

- Doing the right thing

- Missing someone/Grief

- Whether to try something new

- Patching up old hurts

- Explaining life choices

- Feeling overwhelmed

- Choosing the right life partner

- Whether to make a career or geographical move

Conversation Topics about or with Kids

- Instilling ethics or teaching honesty:

- Discipline versus having patience:

- Age-old challenges: (such as dating, drinking, drugs, bullying, sexual harassment)

- 21st century challenges: (like the Internet, social networking, gaming, sports)

More Difficult Subjects

- When you felt wronged or betrayed:

- When you wronged the other person:

- The things you couldn't understand then but understand now:

- Secrets you kept:

Worksheet: Capturing Past Conversations

Think back on a conversation that you would like to re-create. After each question, fill in responses in the spaces provided. These notes will help you as you start to write your story. If you can go back to the place the conversation happened, do so. Surrounding yourself with the sights, smells, and sounds of a place can help trigger your memories. Spend at least five minutes recalling the situation. Think about:

What was the background of the situation—under what circumstances did the conversation occur?

Was the mood happy, carefree, stressful, grief stricken, or something else?

What were you wearing? What other small details can you recall?

Who started the exchange?

Who normally started such exchanges?

Was there a response to a question that was completely unexpected?

Write a rough draft of the conversation. When you're done, examine it to see if your characters' word choices and speeches are true to life.

Worksheet: Conversations You Wish You'd Had

As with the previous worksheet, fill in your responses to the questions below, then use your notes to write about a conversation you wish you had.

Once you've decided who you want to talk to, think about a situation you wish you could converse about. How do you think this person would feel about the issues or events concerned?

How do you think this person would feel about the personalities involved?

Now, go to a place where you can concentrate without interruption. Spend at least five minutes mentally having your conversation. Bask in it.

After you've immersed yourself in your imaginary conversation, make a few notes.

Start writing while the subject vivid in your mind. As you write, think not only of what would have been said but also of how it would be said or phrased.

My Turn: Conversation in the Car

Sometimes family conversation time is overrated. Take this one on the way to my son's soccer game:

Number 1 son: I wonder if there are other ways to take pills, other than swallowing them. Maybe you could take a pill, if it were really small, by putting it up your nose and snorting it so hard that it would go down your throat.

Number 2 son: That's a really stupid idea.

Number 1 son: I thought you were supposed to be coming to my game to cheer for me because Mom's sick of you calling me stupid—not riding in the car calling me stupid.

Number 2 son: I didn't call you stupid; I said the idea was stupid.

Me: (*trying to make peace and change the subject*) Boys . . .

Number 2 son: (*continuing as if I had not interjected anything into the conversation*) Here's why it's stupid. First, it's gross. Second, it could hurt. Third, it could get stuck there and block your nostril. Fourth, if it got stuck there and you put another one in the other nostril the next day, and it also accidentally got stuck there and then you also accidentally duct-taped your mouth shut, you could die. Fifth, if you sneezed you could shoot it out and hurt someone . . . Hey, wait . . . maybe it's not such a stupid idea.

Hey, wait . . . maybe family conversation time isn't so overrated.

THE GOOD AND
THE BAD—WHAT
ABOUT THE UGLY?

Recording good memories comes easily, and including bad ones, even if it isn't easy, can make sense. But what about the ugly times? Should we include ugly traits of family members, brood over hurtful episodes, and open closets with skeletons in them?

The short answer is "it depends." Obviously, you shouldn't be writing to gain sympathy from your readers or get revenge on your subjects. Beyond that, however, it's not so straightforward. How you're going to handle the ugly stuff really depends on your personality, and making the decision about whether or not to write about such episodes might require a degree of candid self-examination. If you are the honest soul that others come to when they want the unsugared truth, you might want to write truthfully. Tactfully handling the truth, however, will usually be better than handling it bluntly. If you're nonconfrontational by nature, you might choose to leave out things that aren't critical to understanding a person or story, or you might merely allude to them, skipping the litany of who said or did what to whom. You might simply state that a decision was not well received or well understood. If you are a ruminator—someone who has to go through an event countless times in your head before you're at peace with it—it might make more sense to include background, even if it is unpleasant or unseemly. The choice is yours.

My grandmother chose a path that was well suited to her personality. Every story was portrayed through the same rose-colored glasses that she wore throughout her life. Every child was beautiful, her grandchildren were particularly beautiful, and almost everyone was kind. The most hurtful act in her past was only touched on as she explained her mood in the setting of a story. The only downside of her approach is that we don't have an unbiased record of events. This frustrated my mother, who always yearned for more details. For me, however, Grandma's approach was a perfect fit for her personality. What was also a good fit was to have those "left-out" details filled in by my mother, the advocate, who annotated some of the stories in my grandmother's Treasure Chest. That's who *she* was.

Just as some wounds are too severe for the body to heal without scarring, some emotional wounds will inevitably leave a mark. Though we may have healed, the scar remains. This is not necessarily a bad thing. If the scar is viewed as a part of the recovery process, it can become just as much of a sign of healing as it is of hurt. Though difficult when a wound is fresh, if you look at the scars of your past in light of how they helped you move forward in life, you will not only be able to convey the story without ranting or whining, you'll also imbue your story with more meaning. In *Courage and Craft: Writing Your Life into Story*, Barbara Abercrombie explains a key benefit to writing about the ugly times: "And here's the paradox of writing about a bad time: by claiming your story, revisiting it, writing it out, you can also let go of it."[1] When handled with care, including such topics can be cathartic. It can lessen that emotional load you've been carrying around.

So what will your readers get out of you airing your dirty laundry or bringing out the family skeletons? Can't they just connect with you through the happy stories? In an interview, women's memoir coach Matilda Butler gives insight to anyone writing about unpleasant episodes of their past. Though meant for memoir-writers, her response sums up why loved ones might be interested in reading about the low points of our lives:

> I think we read memoir because we want to know how did someone else manage? How do they do what they do? Whether it's positive or whether it's negative, we want to know—these are little mini-role models for us that we can call on when something happens in our life and we say, "Well, my situation is different than that, but wow, this is what she did, and I think I can do something similar." I think that's what is so powerful about memoirs. They have the power to influence other people's lives.[2]

When others understand our past, they feel a stronger connection to us. In addition, loved ones gather wisdom from our experiences that might help them navigate or persevere later in life.

Cushioning with Humor

Your best tools in dealing with difficult subjects are tact, humor, and a good thesaurus. If you are trying to find your way around saying your uncle was an ogre, you can say he was cantankerous, passionate, quick-tempered, irascible, surly, or cranky. If he was short as well, you can borrow my grandmother's words and say that he was "as short in temper as he was in stature." His personality could have been overbearing or forceful, but using a humorous euphemism will help convey to the reader that you cared about your relative despite any imperfections. You uncle may have been "a force to be reckoned with when angered" rather than "perpetually wound too tight."

Knowing your audience will also help you gauge the amount of humor and honesty that you can employ. If your grandmother's sister was a complete loon and everyone in the family is open and honest about it, you can refer to her as such. If it wasn't well accepted or if such things are not openly addressed in your family, you might just refer to her as having a few "somewhat bizarre eccentricities."

Avoiding Harm

In my opinion, there are two basic rules: No Whining and Do No Harm. After that, though, there still seems to be a rather fine line of what to include. If a description of an event or incident is likely to cause someone pain or re-ignite a flame of anger that has long been extinguished, give leaving it out some weighty consideration. Alternatively, if you can find a way to allude to the incident without causing hurt, go forward. It's a delicate balance between the need to be honest in your writing and the need to avoid causing pain or reopening old wounds.

Of course, there's a flip side of Do No Harm. Sometimes sharing extremely ugly stories can help others. Survivors of domestic violence and incest are often quite reluctant to bear their wounds, but when they do, they find that their stories empower other victims. Stories of mental illness are also hard to write about, but they can foster understanding when they are shared. Obviously, the amount of consideration you give to sharing painful episodes of your past will have a direct correlation to the magnitude of their unpleasantness.

Examine Your Motives

Perhaps an even more important litmus test is that of your personal motivation. Hold your memories and hurt up to the light and examine your motive for recounting the tale. If there is any vindictiveness involved, put that memory on the back burner until you can approach writing it in a more healthy light. You can unveil your writing when you feel more confident of your motivation.

Editing

Of course, editing is the ultimate filter. You can write your story, then read and appraise the finished piece. You may choose to expound, rephrase, or summarize. In many cases, the simple elimination of details can mitigate the degree of ugliness portrayed and transform the tone of your writing. Once you've written the story or outlined the salient points, then decide if the details are critical to the meat and meaning of your story. Putting yourself in your reader's place as you edit will help you determine what details are pertinent, helpful, and even, loath though we sometimes are to admit it, petty. Memoir writing coach Kendra Bonnett explains, "That's the editing process. . . . You can get it out of your system and then decide it doesn't really add to your story. And just decide to dump it. . . . If nothing else, it might be a healthy, healing process for you."[3]

Writing first and using editing as a filter later least impedes the processes of writing and facing the difficult circumstances that gave rise to your piece. Sometimes you just have to go ahead and put the words on paper before you actually know how you feel about them. This is your past. Go ahead and write about it. Only you can decide if you're going to put Band-Aids over the warts, expose them to the world, or crop them out of the picture entirely.

Additional Tools:

Worksheet: Writing about Difficult Times guides you through identifying difficult memories and the perspective you've gained from them.

My Turn: Grandma and Me shows how my parents worked to protect me from my grandmother's emotional illness.

1. Ibid, 64.
2. Kendra Bonnett and Matilda Butler, "Interview on Writing Your Memoir—Part 4," William Victor, S.L. (2010), accessed December 2, 2011, http://www.creative-writing-now.com/writing-your-memoir.html.
3. Ibid.

Worksheet: Writing about the Difficult Times

Step 1: Identification

Is there a difficult period of history that you've lived through or witnessed? These might include:

- Experiences during armed conflict
- Racism, discrimination, segregation, or other prejudice
- Witnessing violent social events

Is there an "ugly" chapter of your personal history that you've struggled to come to terms with? These might include:

- Physical abuse or assault
- Psychological abuse
- Mental or emotional illness
- Chronic, debilitating, or potentially terminal illnesses
- Relationship problems and heartbreak
- Witnessing individual acts of violence
- Crisis of faith
- Bullying
- Making a particularly hard decision

Step 2: Perspective

With a topic from the previous section in mind, respond to the following questions. After you've finished, you should have a better idea about whether or not you want to write about this topic and how you want to frame it.

Have you healed or risen above these circumstances? If so, how?

How do you continue to cope with this situation or the scars, emotional or otherwise, that resulted from it?

Were you forced to accept and adjust to a new reality? How so?

Are any of your loved ones at risk for similar painful episodes due to their situations or genes? How will telling your story help or empower them?

What do you want your loved ones or readers to take away from this story?

Is there anyone who is going to feel hurt when they read what you've written? Why will they feel hurt?

What do you honestly think motivates you to tell this story?

My Turn: Grandma and Me

I'm not a particularly good judge of character, but there's a silver lining in that. If I had been a good judge of character as a little girl, surely I would have caught on to the fact that my paternal grandmother didn't particularly like me.

I'm not exaggerating or being overly sensitive. It's just a fact. In the '60s, no one talked about mental or emotional illnesses, but we now believe that Grandma suffered from one or more of these. Her mental illness manifested itself in part by her unhealthy attachment to her only child, my father. She never accepted my mother, who "took him away." Likewise, she loved her first grandchild, my sister, to the point of nearly smothering her, but never accepted her second, me, after I was born four hours away from her Virginia home.

Visits to Virginia, especially after my grandpa died, always seemed to stress my parents. I now realize that, aided by my natural obliviousness, they must have done backflips to shield me from Grandma's inequities. They practiced retail therapy, distracting my sister and me from the strained relationship by making K-Mart outings for Barbie paraphernalia when we were visiting. Those outings are fond memories.

As I got older, Grandma became more forgetful and eccentric. She told us, repeatedly, the story of how her mother died when she was six and how her father chose not to raise her. She only knew his last name and couldn't remember much about the orphanage. We figured her lack of family growing up was what made her so protective of her time with my dad. However, it didn't prepare me to be totally rejected by her.

When I was about thirteen, my dad and I drove to Virginia to visit her. I had dressed up for the occasion. Upon seeing me, she insisted that I wasn't her granddaughter. She accused me of being my father's girlfriend and refused to let me in her house.

Only recently, years after her and my father's deaths, have I gained insight into that rejection. Through U.S. Census records, I found out that she misled us about her childhood. Her mother did die when she was six, but her father did not reject her. He and his teenage bride continued to raise her. Far from an orphan, she had four siblings and seven half-siblings.

I wonder if she was living in the past that day and confused me for that teenage bride her father brought home. I wonder what happened in her life that caused her to sever all her connections to her family and lie about their existence. Did her mental illness cause her to deny her roots, or did something in her past trigger or exacerbate her mental disorder?

One day, I believe, I'll meet Grandma again in heaven. We'll have quite a bit of catching up to do.

OTHER WRITINGS

If you've had previous occasions to write pieces that were or became important to you, consider including them in your Treasure Chest. Whether an essay, a letter to an editor, a short story, speech, or eulogy at a funeral, if it gives the reader a connection to something that weighed heavy on your soul, it will be appreciated in times to come.

If you feel that a particular piece is too personal or too private to include, another option is to write about the process. For instance, instead of reproducing a letter that was extremely difficult to write, you might write a reflection called "The Hardest Letter I Ever Wrote."

Are there letters, announcements, or essays you've written that deserve inclusion? If so, search them out and let your loved ones see that side of you.

Additional Tools:

Worksheet: Idea Bank for Other Writings will help you identify other writings that warrant inclusion in your Treasure Chest.

My Turn: Rosemary's Legacy is a devotional piece about the physical imperfections in the body of Christ.

Worksheet: Idea Bank for Other Writings

The following list should help you as you think back to times you've had occasion to put thoughts into writing. Keep in mind that it's not too late—if you see something here that gives you an idea, go for it!

- Schoolwork: (papers, essays, reports, and so on)

- Autobiographical pieces: (like autobiographies—even from 5th grade, resumes, and college applications)

- Devotions or spiritual musings:

- Storytelling or fiction: (including short stories, plays, poems, novels, or even photo album pictures with thoughtful or comedic captions)

Letters

- Love letters to lovers, boy- or girlfriends, or spouses, both past and present:

- Letters to children:

- Letters to parents or grandparents:

- Letters to the family of a deceased loved one:

- Thank-you notes and cards:

Also, think about why you've written:

Pieces Written for a Reason

- Expressing yourself: (for instance, blogs, newsletters, diaries, personal or travel journals)

- Honoring someone: (obituaries, eulogies, introductions, welcome or farewell speeches, thank-you letters, book forewords, letters of recommendation or commendation, and so on)

- Addressing a wrong: (reports or letters to editors, government, school boards, and such)

- Ponderings or "What if?" writings and musings:

- Offering clarity: (memos or other correspondence written to clarify an issue within your organization; journal entries with private thoughts intended to help you process your feelings; expressions of grief or outrage; and so forth)

- Exploring or addressing ethical/moral dilemmas:

- Facilitating social justice: (writings about doing the right thing or discerning the need for action; lobbying materials, and so on)

- Expressing your political and other views: (such as opinion pieces, debate transcripts, and support papers)

- Pieces written for poetry or creative writing contests:

- Faith-related documents: (such as statements of faith, confessions, blessings, or prayers)

My Turn: Rosemary's Legacy

*First published in 1ˢᵗ Presbyterian of Farmington's "Daily Words of Faith,"
2006.*

"From Him [Christ] the whole body, joined and held together by every
supporting ligament, grows and builds itself up in love, as each part does
its work." (Ephesians 4:16, New International Version)

Lately, as I tread firmly on the path of middle age, the symbolism of
the body of Christ has developed more meaning for me. I can think of
many parts of my own body that ache or trouble me, need to be firmed,
reduced, tucked, or, at the minimum, covered. Parts that were at one time
a gift, are, quite frankly, in the way. I often think of us in the body of
Christ exhorting one another to do better, be stronger, go one step further,
or perfect ourselves, just as we attempt to whip our own bodies into a more
acceptable shape.

One day during church, when a hymn reminded me of my recently
departed parents, I learned a new lesson on the body of Christ. As I fought
to hide my tears and compose myself to leave, a longtime church member,
Rosemary, grabbed me, hugged me, and admonished me, "Don't you ever
try to hide your tears in church! We're family!"

So, according to Rosemary, my role in the body of Christ that day was
to emit tears and snot. Furthermore, nobody wanted to put a Band-Aid on
that part, nor should I have felt like covering it.

I was, very simply, a "just as I am" or "come as you are" part of the body
of Christ. As such, any function I was able to fill that day was beautiful and
acceptable before God and my brothers and sisters in Christ.

Wow! That sounds a lot like acceptance to me. If Rosemary was right,
as we age, our bodies are teaching us a lesson on Christian unity. Somehow, in this paradoxical thing called love, we are to not only exhort our
members to stretch themselves to new limits, but when these same members are ailing or failing, we are to support them and accept them without
judgment or resentment.

If the body of Christ can have laugh wrinkles, maybe I can make peace
with my own.

Prayer:

*Father, firstly and foremost, we praise and thank you for our members that
are able to teach and guide us. Help us to acknowledge that we are sometimes
serving you when we feel we are the least capable of service.*

Part 3

The Finer Points

My goal is to assist you as you establish a rich endowment of memories, not to teach the art of writing. There is, however, no denying that this process does involve writing. To push you toward or into such an undertaking without pointing out a few of the larger pitfalls and obstacles would be remiss, possibly setting you up for frustration.

The writing topics that follow will provide you with ways of avoiding some of major potholes (construction delays might be a better metaphor) of writing. As you consider each of them, keep in mind that in this handbook, we are only scratching the surface. You can delve much deeper into these themes through local classes and other resources.

LANGUAGE—GATEKEEPER OF PLACE AND TIME

The patterns of speech that we use define us. It follows, then, that you can keep the characters of the past alive by faithfully recording the speech they used.

Here's where we get to ignore the voice of the English teacher in our head urging us to correct spoken speech patterns as we commit them to paper. Whether your subject's speech was grammatically correct or not, preserving their speech helps you preserve their memory.

While you may want to be stingy in your applications of *gonna* and *wanna*, preserving choice figures of speech, slang words, or regional speech patterns, enriches your stories just as much as using descriptive words. This becomes even more important when you try to capture personalities through direct or indirect quotations.

Clues to Age and Background

The words used by our loved ones can indicate their age, the time in which they lived, and the region of the country in which they grew up. It can even give us a hint as to their education and vocation. For instance, my grandmother used the terms *cook room* and *home place*. *Cook room* takes you back to a time when the kitchen wasn't the center of the house or a place where homework was done but a room dedicated to cooking, canning, and all the messiness inherent to those activities. The *home place* was not the home in which she raised her children, but her husband's family home. These terms reveal much about her background, allowing readers to infer what generation she came from as well as her socioeconomic status.

Likewise, local speech patterns add a regional flavor. Here in the Detroit area, folks grew up drinking *Vernor's*, not ginger ale, just as in the South saying you want a *Coke* does not necessarily mean you want a Coca-Cola.

Individual Speech Patterns

Pictures and images can show what a person looked like. Word usage will convey what they were like. By preserving the speech of your loved ones, you are giving them a chance to do a little character development for themselves.

When you write about others, maintain their inclinations to use understatements, formal speech, or other creative forms of self-expression. For instance, my sister, like our father before her, enjoys twisting her tongue around erudite-sounding phrases. Instead of saying, "or something like that," she'll say, "or some similarly named institution." When I write about her, preserving this habit will allow the reader more insight into her personality than telling them what her profession is or what advanced degrees she holds.

Idiosyncratic pronunciations can be stories in themselves. For instance, as a child, I often mispronounced *thirsty*. I also tended to get parched a few minutes after bedtime. To get a drink of water out of the kitchen, I had to pass through the den where my parents watched television. When I explained my intentions, it would sound like I was saying, "I'm *Thursday*." They never tired of telling me what days of the week *they* were. That probably explains why, whenever I heard my dad's Virginian pronunciation of *afraid* (a-fred), I always gleefully responded that I was "a-Sam," or "a-George."

Grammar, or lack thereof, can also mirror a person's personality, education, and their general art of personal expression. In what would otherwise be a somewhat dry genealogical reference book, author Robert Hedgcock peppers *The Hitchcock, Hedgecock, Hedgcock Family in Maryland and North Carolina and Their Descendants* with one family member's verbatim recollections. Not only does he preserve her expressions of "a might early," "youngins," and "spinnin' tales," but he maintains her run-on sentences. I feel like I am in the room with Robert and Keziah Hedgcock when I read, "We only had a log hut to live in when Benedict was born cause we had just got to North Carolina in '77 and he came a might early the first week we were here."[1]

You'll notice that Hedgcock was able to convey personality without resorting to phonetic spellings. That's not only simpler for the writer; it's easier for the reader. As we read and track through a paragraph, coming upon uncommon spellings can trip us up and slow us down. Though it's sometimes nice to give the reader a sample, maintaining such spellings through an entire piece of writing can actually detract from the story itself.

Regardless of what method you use, conserving personality through your characters' speech will make your writing more interesting. When the writing is varied and your characters' individuality breaks through, the reader, no longer so sure of what to expect, becomes re-engaged. Although you may find yourself having to explain some uncommon or irregular uses of language, you'll also find it worth the effort—it will produce rich, luscious images for your readers to devour.

Additional Tools:

Worksheet: Brainstorming Colloquial and Idiomatic Words and Expressions helps you identify and preserve your loved ones' speech patterns.

Writing Exercise: Preserving Language guides you through incorporating loved ones' speech patterns into your memory narratives.

My Turn: God Bless America provides a glimpse of my mother's speech under trying circumstances.

1. Robert Hedgcock, *The Hitchcock Hedgecock Hedgcock Family in Maryland and North Carolina and Their Descendants*, 2nd ed., (Utica, KY: McDowell Publications, 2000), 19.

Brainstorming Colloquial and Idiomatic Words and Expressions

What are the random things that your family members say? Brainstorm about who says what below.

Nouns: (such as *kicks* for *shoes* or *grub* for *food*)

Proper Nouns: (calling a son *Junior* or *Brother*, and names for officials, pastors, God, and so on)

Verbs: (such as *fixing to*, *rile up*, *reckon*, and so forth)

Adjectives: (such as *catty-wampus*, *uppity*, and *sweet*)

Expressions: (Such as *darn tootin'*, *aye*, and so on)

Writing Exercise: Preserving Language

Step 1:

Think about a memory of loved one.

As you make your word choices, consider the following, and jot yourself some notes:

Expressions your loved one used common to most people in the region in which they lived or previously lived: (such as *Y'all*, *you guys*, or *youins*)

Speech patterns originating from an accent, affecting the way a loved one pronounced common words: (*a-fred* instead of *afraid*, *yellow* instead of *hello*, and so on)

Speech pattern that originated from a particular time period: (*ice-box*, *oleo*, and so on)

Euphemisms—expressions used in lieu of expressions that might be considered impolite—or lack thereof: (such as "I gotta go see a man about a dog" or "digging for gold")

Step 2:

If you can't think of a scenario you want to write about, recall or imagine your loved one going to great lengths to avoid engaging in an activity such as riding a roller coaster, going to church, attending the theatre, or playing sports. Through some turn of events, your loved one ends up realizing that they have to do the thing they dread. In doing so, they find that the dreading was the bad part and the activity was bearable or even enjoyable.

Close your eyes for a moment and visualize this individual.

After you have him or her firmly in your thoughts, imagine the circumstances.

Now write the story from that person's perspective, keeping his or her individual use of language in mind.

Step 3:

As they say on the shampoo bottles, rinse and repeat. Clear your thoughts, choose another friend or family member, visualize, imagine, and write.

My Turn: God Bless America!

My mother hated swearing. She especially hated it if she herself was tempted to swear, so she'd say "God bless America!" instead. When I was little, Mom sewed clothes for my sister and me. More often than not, the dresses would turn out beautifully, but Mom had a love-hate relationship with her machine and the craft itself. We'd know to steer clear of that end of the house when we heard the yells of "God bless America!"

When she was sorely tempted, "God bless America!" would be interjected adamantly as an adjective, resulting in somewhat comical yet emphatic expressions. One particularly memorable utterance came when my cat, who was in the process of weaning a litter of kittens, walked in from outside with a treat for her babies—a rabbit's head. No hint of a lie, after going in for a visual identification of the object the cat was trying to carry through the kitchen, Mom stifled a blood-curling scream, then yelled, "Cat, get that God-bless-America rabbit's head out of my kitchen!"

The cat, never one for following directions to the letter, dropped the rabbit head onto the kitchen floor and beat a trail back out the door and into the yard. That left Mom having to chase her around the yard, demanding that she return to remove the offensive object. America was blessed multiple times.

VOICE—BEING YOURSELF ON PAPER

In writing guides, the term *voice* is most commonly used to indicate whether a composition is written in first person (I) or third person (he, she, or it) with a narrator. There is a second person as well, such as—ahem—in instructional guides, in which the author addresses readers directly, using *you*.

Voice tells us who is speaking. The use of *I* tells us the author is speaking, while *he*, *she*, or *it* tells us that an outside party is narrating the story. Because your Treasure Chest's audience is your loved ones, it's easy to fall into first person voice as we tell our stories. The great majority of sources on writing concur that this is a natural choice for an informal tone. In fact, quite a few writer-coaches contend that the writing itself will be a more powerful conveyor of a firsthand experience if written from an *I* perspective.

However, since a Treasure Chest is a collection, you aren't limited to one voice. You can choose to narrate your memories or knowledge of other people, events, or places in third person. The choice is yours. If you don't have any strong preferences, you might want to start with first person voice.

Language arts experts have another understanding of voice. Again, it tells who is speaking, but this time by projecting a personality or attitude into the piece. It's the writer's way of expressing him- or herself that allows the reader to get a feeling for them, their style, and their state of mind. Writers allow their individuality to shine through their use of voice.

Successful writers caution that it takes many years of experience for a writer to successfully develop voice and style.[1] Without disputing that, I would like to point out that in my area, voice is taught to elementary school students. It not only helps prevent their writing from sounding overly stilted and mechanical but also solidifies the concept of writing as a form of personal expression. Surely, if nine-year-olds can be encouraged to let their personalities shine through in their essays, the hobby memory keeper too can benefit from a little advice.

Through their voice, writers express their mood, their individuality, and even their perspective on their story and subject matter. This means you can convey your conviction or involvement in the subject and connect more deeply with the reader by the way you write. As Treasure Chest writers, we have a natural incentive to exercise our written voice. We're not just leaving a written record of past events; we're forging connections with our loved ones. For this reason, it's doubly important to let your personality shine through in your writing. Happily, the casual tone of a Treasure Chest collection allows a lot of leeway in expression. With this in mind, think about the following points as you write, experiment, and develop your unique voice.

Imitate, But Not Too Much

If you like the writing style of a particular author, you might find it helpful to start out emulating them, particularly if their voice is similar to your own. However, your Treasure Chest needs to represent *you*, so don't overindulge in imitation at the cost of not being yourself. Try writing in the style of the writer you enjoy. After you've worked with this for a while, examine your writing for elements that are not evocative of your personality or that do not resonate with you. These will be the elements that you need to further refine.

Read a Lot

Writers agree, pretty much universally, that reading helps their writing. It stimulates the brain, and as results, ideas flow more easily and they have an easier time putting their stories on paper. You can accomplish the above emulation by reading authors whose style you enjoy.

Indulge Your Imagination as You Relive Your Memory

Spending a few minutes recalling your story will help your writing. This is essentially what you are doing when you brainstorm about a story or build a word bank; you are rehashing the story. Slow down and remember the flow of emotions. Remember what else you saw, smelled, observed, and heard. This will help you convey the essence of the event while wrapping it in highly descriptive text.

Imaginary Friends

Envisioning yourself relating memories to a trusted friend or relative will not only help you get started but will also allow you to resist the urge to write the event to please someone else. Instead of focusing on an undefined (or worse, critical) future audience, focus on telling your story to someone you know will enjoy it.

This helps you keep your readers at the forefront of your mind, and enables you to tell the story simply yet without inhibition, yielding all the accompanying personality of verbally recounting an event to a close friend. You can even use a voice recorder (most smartphones have them now) and tell your story aloud. Better still, tell your story to an actual friend as opposed to an imaginary one. The natural rhythm of your friendship will allow you to foreshadow, embellish, and include any humorous or emotional perspectives.

First Draft as a Letter or Email

Like the method above, recording your first draft as a letter or email can aid you in setting a casual tone and help you write more spontaneously. It is, after all, a first draft. You will edit and hone it later. Just start writing, even badly, to get the story from your long-term memory banks onto paper.

Don't Overedit Yourself

This project is, by definition, egocentric, so it's okay to mention yourself. Make sure you aren't working so hard on writing well that you write yourself out of the stories. Just as preserving the speech patterns of our loved ones will allow us to better portray them, maintaining your own individual writing patterns will make your Treasure Chest read like a story related to an intimate friend. As you edit later, continue to keep your readers in mind. If you like to use phrases that are local or distinct to your family, or if members of your family are not native speakers of the tongue in which you are writing, you might want to go to some lengths to make your use of language universally understandable.

Write to Music

Many authors say that they write better when they write to music. Perhaps it because the music helps them get in the zone. Try this and see if it helps you too.

Do Edit a Little

In advising teachers on how to teach children to inject a strong voice into their writing, educator Beth Newingham suggests that students reread their writing with the following checklist in mind:

> You know writing has voice if:
>> It shows the writer's personality
>> It sounds different from everyone else's
>> It contains feelings and emotions
>> The words come to life
>> It comes from the heart[2]

Once again, if it works for young writers, it can work for us too. Sometimes our stories don't have a lot of emotional content, but they come from the heart, so we can definitely let our personalities shine through.

Trust Yourself

Be yourself on paper and trust that your readers will enjoy the real you. Expert Laura Backes reminds us, "Voice is the simplest writing technique to learn, because it's already in you. But it's the hardest to achieve, because it involves trusting yourself."[3] Although good voice seems difficult to achieve, as you gain self-confidence, your writing will become less inhibited. Once you have developed a rhythm and flow to your stories, let loose and let it shine.

Additional Tools

Writing Exercise: Finding Your Voice helps you let your voice shine throughout your narrative.

Someone Else's Turn: Excerpt from "The Dog and the Trip to South Carolina" is an eleven-year-old's story of a trip in the "jail on wheels."

1. Holly Lisle, "Ten Steps for Finding Your Voice," HollyLisle.com, accessed February 18, 2014, http://hollylisle.com/ten-steps-to-finding-your-writing-voice/.
2. Beth Newingham, "Lesson Plan: Adding Strong Voice to Your Writing," Scholastic Inc., accessed January 19, 2012, http://www.scholastic.com/teachers/lesson-plan/adding-strong-voice-your-writing.
3. Laura Backes, "Tips for Developing an Original Voice," Children's Book Insider, LLC, accessed October 3, 2012, http://write4kids.com/original.html.

Writing Exercise: Finding Your Voice

Step 1: You're going to tell a very simple story. Imagine you went to pay for your lunch yesterday and found that you'd forgotten your wallet. A total stranger volunteers to pay for your meal. Take a couple of minutes and write your story.

Step 2: Now that you have the basic facts of the story down, start telling the story again, but this time, tell it to a child you know quite well. Be sure you include details that children invariably ask about: What did he say? What did you say? Why didn't you have your wallet? Why did he do that?

Step 3: Now you're going to relate the incident to your best buddy or trusted girlfriend. Make sure you include all your reactions.

Step 4: Look back over your process. With any luck, each retelling contained a little more of your personality, your values, and your personal style. If not, try it one more time, endeavoring to tell the story in such a way that the reader, at the end of your narrative, will have a feeling for the type of person you are.

Someone Else's Turn: The Dog and the Trip to South Carolina

By Nathaniel Hedgecock

My son Nathaniel wrote this at age eleven. Reading back over it, I'm pretty sure his assignment stressed the importance of descriptive phrases. Besides a strong voice, you'll also note an uncorrected grammar mistake. This was left intentionally to illustrate how personality can shine through writing in myriad ways.

We had spent fourteen hours in my dad's light blue van, going through endless valleys and in circles around mountainous cliffs and valleys like an endless merry-go-round. The insides of the car were gray and dull, and when we finally arrived at my Aunt Däna's house, we were as relieved as an innocent person in danger of facing life in jail under high security is on the day of his trial after he has been found innocent. We were greeted by my enthusiastic three-year-old cousin, Ellen, and my Aunt Däna walked up behind her. It felt good to be there. It only took ten rest stops, two episodes of throwing up, and fourteen hours of somewhat boring scenery.

My aunt's house was inviting and looked like it came from a fairy tale. The birds chirped tunes and melodies back and forth, and the air smelled like lavender with a hint of rose. We were excited though, and we had great reason to be that way: we were going to see where my mom went to college, (and remember afterwards—I had been there before but I didn't remember it), meet her old college friends, and maybe, if we were lucky, come home with a new family member, a tri-colored springer spaniel. I couldn't wait! But then again, that was in 2003, and we also couldn't wait to see Santa Claus and sit on his lap; I can make a whole list of things we couldn't wait for. . . .

A few days later, it was time to go home. Reluctantly, we said our good-byes and took our new dog back home. I watched the same hills and valleys that were like the answer to one hundred divided by three and go on forever. . . . We got off the highway two days later; I knew I was finally home after another trip in the jail on wheels.

Hugo back in Michigan

HUMOR IS ALMOST ALWAYS WELCOME

It's no secret that people like to laugh. People especially like to laugh at other people's predicaments. Laughing together creates bonds, so preserving past laughter will be a gift to future generations in a variety of ways. Stories can be funny because the situation itself is funny or because the writing describing the situation is funny. It's nice when both happen simultaneously. What we all want to avoid is having the humor in the former eliminated by a lack of ability in the latter. We certainly don't want to kill the humor that is already intrinsic to the memory.

Describing Laughter

Everything I've ever read about humor writings says that you are not supposed to say something is funny. Instead, you should describe the situation in such a way that the reader finds it funny. I personally think we can break that rule for the purposes of a Treasure Chest. We don't have characters; we're telling stories. If the folks in our memory were prone to laughter, then let them laugh in your writing. If it reads unfunny, then try describing their laughter. Note whether they giggle, howl, cackle, or snort. This, by the way, is another instance where the thesaurus can be your best friend. Look up the word that just doesn't quite describe the laughter, and chances are the right one will appear.

Don't Spoil the Punch Line

The unexpected is funnier than the predictable. When something takes us by surprise, it causes us to consider a situation in a new light and can launch us into a lighthearted mood.[1] Like a joke, a narrative is funnier if it ends in an unexpected way. If the memory has an ironic or comedic ending, don't give too much of it away in advance. Leave the funniest part for last. Similarly, if your take on the situation is facetious or satirical, end, rather than start, with your wry thoughts or punch line.

189

Admit Your Embarrassment

Don't bother trying to save face or to make yourself look good. Readers will better relate to embarrassment than to unflappable poise in the face of absolute chaos. If the subject of your story was able to maintain face during an incident, explain at what emotional or mental cost it was upheld.

Keep Others' Feelings in Mind

You can show humor through your descriptions of a plight or predicament, your writing style, or self-depreciation. However, your humor shouldn't come at the cost of someone's feelings. Avoid teasing that is unkind or jokes that will be hurtful to others.

Use Adjectives

A situation that is colorfully described will tickle your readers' funny bones. For instance, a well-dressed gentleman slipping in goop is slightly humorous. However, when that same vain pompous gentleman slips in a vile, malodorous pool of sticky, green gelatinous glop that adhered to his black woolen Armani pants or his starched-stiff cuffs in dark ropy tentacles, it's funnier. Use many colorful, graphic, vivid, expressive, depictive, illustrative adjectives.

Use Comparisons

Many of us edit too much as we write and end up editing our sense of humor out of our writing. When we're telling a story to a good friend or a spouse, we often throw in comparisons to illustrate our stories. We say that a child screamed over the removal of a splinter as if we were conducting a field amputation or that the dog barked and growled as though a giant man-eating squirrel was at the door.

Go ahead and include your natural comparisons as you write your stories—even if they are a tad embellished. You can always fine-tune or eliminate them when you make your edits.

Ending with Humor

You can also lighten a story or its ending with an "I wonder" statement, such as, "I wonder what my sister thought when . . ." to add irony or a lighthearted surprise.

Finding Humor by Perspective

Sometimes the true humor in a situation comes out of the way we look at it, rather than the events or circumstances themselves. The shift in perspective can bring cognitive and emotional relief when dealing with difficult times.

Having a humorous perspective is not always an either-or proposition, and it shouldn't be reserved only for humorous stories. It can also play a role in less joyful occasions. Used appropriately in the face of crisis or tragedy, humor can be conducive to healing. This is because, in the midst of our anguish, it's necessary for us to realize that we will eventually be able to laugh again. When the emotional weight of dealing with a loss seems unbearable, humor gives us a momentary respite from carrying that weight, providing a coping mechanism that allows us to join with others in acknowledging a time beyond our tears.

My family experienced this firsthand at my neighbor's funeral. The rabbi was discussing Larry's achievements, attributes, and hobbies, when he unexpectedly threw in the fact that, though Larry was blessed in many ways, he was particularly unlucky with fast food—no one in the family could remember Larry ever once actually getting what he ordered at McDonald's. The rabbi gave us mourners a beautiful gift. Imagining Larry fondly, with laughter instead of the wrenching pain we knew at the time, muted our grief for just a moment.

The experts at *This Emotional Life* explain the physiological mechanism behind the emotional relief that humor brings: "During times of mirth, the brain also produces endorphins, which raise our pain threshold and can reduce pain we may already be feeling. Mirth also triggers a relaxation response."[2] The humor you provide for your reader, whether in a lighthearted poem or heart-wrenching narrative, gives the reader an actual emotional lift. This enhances the gift you are preparing for your loved ones.

Including humor in such stories also carries literary value. Not only does a hint of humor give literary relief to what would otherwise be a sad, heavy story, but humor can also increase the poignancy of a narrative. Loss has more texture and depth when it is juxtaposed against laughter and joy. Only when you understand the inherent happiness of a situation can you understand the depth of the storm surges that overwhelm it. It's no surprise, therefore, that often the most moving, touching stories are ones that have us laughing through our tears. The opposite is also true. A moment of levity can sometimes be appreciated even more in view of the deplorable circumstances from which it sprang.

Some situations do not seem even the slightest bit funny when they are happening but later bloom into hilarity. We often hear a humorous story beginning with the phrase, "Though I didn't find it funny at the time." When such situations involve our children, for instance, they are not funny when they happen because of the gravity of raising our kids and teaching them not to do harebrained things. The fear that they will continue to be harebrained and, as result, not enjoy happy, successful lives, weighs heavily on us. Once the kids have become successful adults, that burden is lifted, and we can laugh gleefully.

Other times, our wounded pride, psyche, or whatever other body part we landed on has to heal before we think something is funny. Psychologists call this emotional distance. From the center of the situation, it appears that nothing funny is going on, but once we see the situation from afar, we gain a new perspective and see the humor involved.

There is a time to be funny and a time to grieve. Be aware of times and events from which loved ones may never have enough emotional distance to see in a comedic light. Other episodes may become funny with time, but until enough time has passed to achieve emotional distance, a humorous handling of those situations will land flat.

Chances are that as you write about some difficult moments, your sense of humor will peek through. As editor-in-chief, you can hone that humor or keep your writing serious. Just make sure your Treasure Chest isn't closed to laughter.

Additional Tools:

Worksheet: Identifying Humor not only helps you identify humorous episodes but also helps your humor shine through in your storytelling.

My Turn: Christmas Eve Debacle provides a humorous account of one of my kids' worst moments.

1. "This Emotional Life: Humor," NOVA/WGBH Science Unit and Vulcan Productions, Inc. (2009), accessed November 1, 2011, http://www.pbs.org/thisemotional-life/topic/humor/humor.
2. Ibid.

Worksheet: Identifying Humor

Embarrassing Moments (that aren't too private to report)

Think back on embarrassing moments. (Hint: look back at your "Lessons Learned" brainstorming sheets for ideas.) Consider also including:

Embarrassments on the sports field: (running the wrong way, scoring on yourself, and so on)

Embarrassments meeting the in-laws:

Embarrassments hosting parties or business meetings:

Embarrassment caused by children: (church comes to my mind)

Wardrobe malfunctions: (two different shoes, shirt inside out, or mismatched socks)

Foot-in-mouth embarrassment:

Anecdotes

Think of a humorous anecdote. Write down the bare facts of what happened.

Now brainstorm descriptive words or phrases that might enhance the humor of the situation. This can include nouns and phrases, like *hissy-fit* for tantrum.

Add any aspects of personalities that might increase the humor of the situation. Remember, you don't have to end up looking or smelling like a rose.

Add any reactions that other people were having to the situation. Be sure to jot down any additional amusing descriptors.

Now construct your opening sentence in such a way that you don't give the punch line.

Finally, construct an ending sentence that will give your readers a surprise.

My Turn: Christmas Eve Debacle

There's an old adage in Germany—or maybe just with the colleagues I worked with—that, roughly translated, says, "If you can't serve in any other way, you can always serve as a bad example."

While serving as the candle-lighting family in church one Christmas, our family ended up serving as the all-time bad example.

Two men of action or double trouble?

The first Christmas season after the deaths of my parents in a car accident was difficult. Hoping to stave off feelings of grief and loss, my sister, husband, and I decided to start a new tradition. Instead of attending the brief "loud and noisy" (family and children's) Christmas Eve service, we would take part in the later communion service. We were to be the candle-lighting family, which involved reading a litany and a prayer while lighting the candles on the Advent wreath. My sister and I even volunteered to sing a little a cappella duet.

In anticipation of our role, I dressed our boys, ages two and five, in adorable coordinating outfits, and we adults did the best we could with what we had. My eldest, Nathaniel, had lines to say and was well practiced. As public speaking, not to mention singing, was outside of my comfort zone, I was a bundle of nerves.

When the time came, we started the duet too high or too low (I can't remember which), but we muddled through. My five-year-old said his part, we adults said our parts, and my husband dutifully lit the candles with the big brass candle-lighting dubbie. My youngest, Joshua, seemed content to watch it all from his perch on my hip. It all appeared to be going smoothly. As it turns out, appearances can be deceiving.

Beginning to relax, just before I started to read the longish ending prayer, I put Joshua down. Big mistake. Joshua, apparently, wasn't very moved or awestruck by the proceedings and thought the thing to liven up the party was to run wild circles around the communion table that stood front and center of the chancel. I say *apparently* because he proceeded to do so right as I began the prayer. He was also, apparently, enjoying himself, if the mirthful chortles emanating from him were anything by which to judge. I continued to read the prayer, albeit in a trembling voice. I was praying all right.

My husband was stuck behind my sister, unable to reach Joshua without bowling her over. I snuck a peak at her. She was stifling a grin as she gave me an "I'm-not-the-one-that-went-forth-and-procreated" look. A sneak peak at the pastor was no more rewarding. Outwardly appearing to be praying with his eyes shut, he somehow let me know that snagging a preschooler as he ran by was not in his job description or pay grade. Time slowed to a crawl. I continued to read the prayer aloud as I prayed an altogether different prayer silently. Playing to his audience, Joshie continued his jubilant running.

If I had managed one, a sneak peak at my five-year-old might have clued me in that he was also finding the lack of adult intervention appalling. It might also have warned me that Nathaniel was poised to take action. Good man, he, to have in a crisis. The gleeful circling tot had to be stopped. The situation called for nothing less than a flying tackle.

Nathaniel let his brother go by him and then, in a display of exquisite timing, launched himself, flattening his brother behind the communion table. Their struggling, intertwined bodies stayed there until the approximate time of the "Amen." Their flailing legs, however, could be seen by all. "All" should have had their eyes closed, but this entertainment was an early Christmas present—a gift from God, as it were. Joshua managed to free himself from his older brother as I read the final "Amen." He ran front and center of the chancel and punctuated the "Amen" with a little jig, just like a football player does after scoring the winning touchdown.

Prayer finished, we collected our offspring (*spawn* was the word that came to mind at the time), and slunk into a pew. I was certain I'd have to change churches, change towns, change everything, but we didn't. We were, however, excused from further candle-lighting-family duties until Joshua was twelve. Joshua's seventeenth year has come and gone. We haven't been asked.

ENDINGS

It's difficult to say whether it is harder to get started or to end. Many of these stories are so near and dear to our hearts that they almost write themselves. Almost, that is, until it comes to ending the piece. If the story has a natural surprise ending, you're all set. However, if your story is stubborn and hasn't volunteered to write itself, much less provide you with a provocative ending or twist, here are a few basic tips that I have found distinctly helpful.

Save the Best for Last

Just as the most emphatic or most important word of your sentence makes a larger impact when it occurs at the end of the sentence, many authors feel that the impact of the story should also come at the end. Thus, they advise you not to give away too much of your story too early. As discussed in the humor section, this is definitely the case when you're hoping to give your readers a laugh.

Save the best—whether it's a lesson, punch line, quote, or question—for last. For example, instead of titling a story "The First Time I Met my Brother-in-Law" you could describe your chance meeting with an individual. As the story finishes, you could reveal that, as fate would have it, this individual turned out to be your future brother-in-law.

Irony

If there is an intrinsic irony or unexpected turn in a story or situation—or if your take on the story is ironic—reveal the irony in your ending. When we go to the movies to see an adventure film, we love it when the plot takes an unexpected turn. We love being surprised. You can achieve a similar result when writing about a situation that ends quite differently than the reader would otherwise expect. A touch of foreshadowing—alluding to what is to come—can heighten the irony. Examine your memories and narratives with this in mind.

Be Definitive—or Not

You might not always want your readers to reach a point of complete understanding. Many times, we are writing to persuade, explain, convince, or memorialize, but that's not always the case. Though we often have a clear idea of what we want the reader to end up thinking, sometimes we just want to leave our readers with something to chew on mentally.

If you don't have a point or place at which you want your reader to arrive, you can leave them thinking or wondering. There's nothing wrong with that. Well-known authors agree that writers don't have to leave readers knowing what to think or feel. In fact, giving them a laugh or something to contemplate makes your writing resonate. Some of the most effective endings are questions posed to the reader. A simple example is closing with a question, such as "what would *you* have done?"

Show, Don't Tell

Sometimes it pays not to summarize, at least not too much. Make sure you allow your story to reveal itself naturally. If a lesson has been learned, a character has grown, or an epiphany been achieved, bring that out through your narrative. This will help your memories come to life and will prevent your stories from seeming contrived. Your readers can then draw their own conclusions without you having to lead them.

Why This Memory Matters

Your readers will not only want to know what happened in your past, but also what you gained from your experience. They will wonder why a particular memory matters to you or has stuck in your mind. Explaining a story's significance works particularly well in a Treasure Chest collection. When you describe how your experience changed your perspective or influenced future decisions, you're deepening your connection with your readers. So, as you write, allow loved ones insight into how you and others felt about the events you narrate.

Additional Tools:

Worksheet: Editing Your Ending guides you through a review of your writing to improve your endings.

My Turn: No Comprendo has an ending with a twist.

Worksheet: Editing Your Ending

Examine a memory or story you have written. Consider the following, jot down notes, and edit where necessary.

Does this story have a conflict? If so, has your writing resolved that conflict?

Has your ending left your readers wondering about what comes next? This is fine if you want a good segue into a subsequent piece, but otherwise revise so that your readers won't be dissatisfied. (You can leave readers with something to think about, but most won't appreciate being left on the edge of a cliff wondering what happened next.)

Have you taken your reader to some sort of realization? Better yet, have you taken them to an unexpected realization? (This isn't always necessary, but be alert for opportunities that lend themselves to this.)

Would some sort of twist work at the end? (Again, this isn't always necessary, but it's great when you can do it.)

Last Look:

Now that you've edited, reread your piece with the following in mind:

Does it sound contrived? Make sure you haven't worked too hard and removed the normal flow of the story.

Does your voice still come through? Does it sound like something you would normally say? Make sure you haven't edited your own personality out of it.

My Turn: No Comprendo

When my kids were little, I tried my best to be a good parent. (I still do.) I was extremely diligent—possibly even to a fault. I used car seats, sunscreen, and time-outs and provided balanced meals, fresh air, exercise, and many play dates. When it came to TV and videos, I allowed only a limited amount of PBS and Animal Planet and even got them Christian videos starring animated vegetables, which taught Bible stories and ethics with humor. The vegetables were also very diverse—a couple even spoke Spanish.

In retrospect, it seems that my youngest paid more attention to the Spanish and humor than to the ethic and morals.

During my son's fourth birthday party, several little girls began drawing mermaids on the driveway with sidewalk chalk. The birthday boy began adding chicken pox to all the mermaids, which was bringing the little girls close to tears. (Apparently, mermaids are not supposed to have any complexion issues or communicable diseases. Who knew?) Deciding the nip the problem in the bud, I lifted my son onto a bench and began scolding him. "Joshua," I said, "you *do* realize, don't you, that even though it is your birthday, you can still get a time-out?"

He looked me straight in the eye and said, without cracking a grin, "*No comprendo.*"

Since no adult could look him in the face after that, Joshua never did get that time-out. I don't remember what happened with the mermaids.

Part 4

Deeper Reflections

There's a reason our first diaries come with a lock and key. For most of us, sharing our more vulnerable side—let alone our most personal thoughts and stories—does not come easily or naturally. We're much more comfortable sharing an overall picture of our lives than we are with sharing the personal stories that helped get us there.

However, it's precisely the more private stories of personal growth that connect our loved ones to our journeys. One of my all-time favorite plays illustrates this point. In *Quilters*, each character, an American pioneer woman, has been given a bag of scraps from which to make a quilt. Regardless of the quality of their scraps, each character made a quilt, and each square of the quilt represented an event in their lives. Through the characters' explanations of their squares, the audience learns about their private battles and the obstacles they have overcome. These characters, like many of us, were able to make something useful and beautiful from scraps and personal tragedies. Hearing each character tell her story was touching because of the daunting measure of openness that sharing required.

Those of us who are relatively private can be fairly open about the final quilt we have made of our lives, but we are loathe to reveal the processes we have gone through to make that quilt, much less tout around the original fabric scraps from which our quilts originated. Others have no idea if we've followed the pattern we chose early on or if we had to drastically alter our design to accommodate events in our lives.

If that's your preference and personality, should you just go with your instincts? Obviously, that's an individual decision, but I urge you to consider moving out of your comfort zone and revealing a little more of yourself than comes naturally. Why? Because leaving a legacy of our final-product selves without any insight to our previous work-in-progress selves is akin to leaving a description of a treasure without the accompanying map—no one gets a close-up view of the true treasure. Only our very closest family and friends—those who were in positions to observe our journey—truly understand us. For the youth in our lives, we are an enigma. They are just starting the process of piecing their quilts together, and they are hard-pressed to imagine their own quilts looking like ours. By revealing more of ourselves in our writing, we are not only given others a clearer perspective of how we constructed our squares during given circumstances, but we are also offering up helpful wisdom to those still in the process of piecing their lives together.

The following sections will walk you through ideas to consider as you write about deeper reflections and your own vulnerabilities. You don't have to give away the key to your diary, but contemplate letting your loved ones have a glimpse of a page or two.

LETTERS TO CHILDREN

When my children were small, my husband and I had wills drawn up. Legally, we were prepared for nearly every eventuality, but what would our children know of us if the unthinkable did happen? My husband chose to trust that the unthinkable wouldn't happen. Not being capable of such trust, I chose to write each of my children a letter to be given to them when they were old enough to understand the contents.

In the meantime, my kids have grown into teenagers, and I have probably told them all the things that are important for them to understand. They might even understand me better than I understood myself at the time. Those letters have remained unread, except by me, for well over a decade now. I admit that writing these letters was a difficult activity, albeit a cathartic one. Difficult or not, though, I'm contemplating writing another for each of them as they approach adulthood.

I'm not advising you to sit down and contemplate your own mortality to motivate yourself to put some thoughts on paper for your children. Just think about the things that you really want them to know and the things you think are important for them to hear or see in black and white. Perhaps they're the same things you've been saying for years but that you fear have gotten lost amongst all the other conversations, scoldings, naggings, and hurryings to and from. Perhaps they're the things that may have been lost in the passing of years. If your children are very young, you might record your hopes and dreams for them. You could even consider it more of a time capsule through writing, or a letter explaining what you hope they understand when they look back on your parenting. If your children are grown, perhaps it will be a summary of what they have meant to you, what they have taught you, and what they are still teaching you.

Writing letters to children is not for everyone, but it can be a way of bridging chasms, expressing the thoughts and feelings that are hard to say, and generally crystallizing the things you love about your child and the happiness and aspirations you hope for them. It can also be a great tradition to pass on. Try it as an exercise. If it's successful, leave it in your Treasure Chest. Your children may cherish it deeply. Knowing your dreams for them may give them confidence as they go about dreaming their own dreams.

Additional Tools:

Worksheet: Letters to Children assists you as you consider what you want to say to your child or children.

My Turn: Mother to Daughter provides a different slant on a mother-to-daughter letter.

Worksheet: Letters to Children

Step 1:

Start by building a word bank about a child's personality qualities. Circle the words that pertain to your child and add your own descriptive words.

- Adventurous

- Affectionate

- Athletic

- Book-lover

- Careful

- Caring

- Cautious

- Cheerful

- Compassionate

- Cooperative

- Decisive

- Easy-going

- Empathetic

- Exuberant

- Funny

- High-strung

- Impulsive

- Introspective

- Intuitive

- Loving

- Nature-lover

- Observant

- Opinionated

- Patient

- Quiet

- Sensitive

- Smart

- Social

- Spontaneous

- Talkative

Your own words:

Step 2:

Now think carefully (and jot down notes) about the following:

- What is it about this child that makes him or her special, even unique?

- What types of qualities did they exhibit from youngest childhood, and which qualities developed later?

- Which of this child's qualities will help (or has helped) him or her go far in life?

- Beyond the obvious joys of loving a child, how has this child changed your own life? What has this little person taught you?

- What dreams do you have for this child?

Step 3:

With these thoughts in mind, go ahead and start a rough draft. After you've finished, let it sit for a while and develop (kind of like letting a good bread dough rise). Look at your notes again before going back and editing what you've written.

My Turn: Mother to Daughter

As my teenagers would not be terribly thrilled with my most personal thoughts about them being published, I've chosen to include a blog post I wrote wherein I imagined getting a letter from my mother. It's as much an illustration of "Conversations from the Past" as "Letters to Children," but I trust you'll get the idea.

I recently tried to comfort a friend as she mourned the sudden loss of her mother. She lamented, "She's always the one I call when I want the truth. I've always counted on her honesty. Now what am I going to do?" I found myself saying words that I didn't even know were in my mind or heart. Yet as I spoke them, I knew them to be true. I told her that she has all her mother's advice, encouragement, and honesty still within her. Her mother has always been an honest confidant, loving friend, and outright cheering section. Her relationship with her mother was so strong that she doesn't need to pick up the phone to hear what her mother has to say. When her mother was alive, she called her mother knowing what her mother would say, even when it wasn't really what she thought she wanted to hear. Death doesn't just erase that.

Now the conversation keeps running back through my head and creeping up behind me. Does that apply to my mother, too? My mother has been gone for years. She died way before I was anywhere near done asking her questions about child rearing. Do I know, intrinsically, what she would say? I often long to be allowed just one last phone call. Perhaps better still would be getting a letter, like the following, that I could read over and over.

Dear Laura,

I wish your father and I could tell you how proud we are of the woman you have become. We notice that you still struggle with your self-esteem, and it baffles us. You are such a good person, good mother, and wonderful wife. As far as the housekeeping is concerned, well, at least you come by any lacks in that department honestly. It's not the type of thing that really matters anyway. Remember how I used to make y'all clean up for the cleaning lady so she wouldn't think badly of us? Such a waste of emotional energy!

I love watching the boys grow. I wish I could be there to let them know that I watch. In many ways, they are still just as they were at the time of the auto accident—still Pete and "RePete." Don't get discouraged when they squabble. You and your sister did it, and Uncle Joe used to tease me mercilessly. They still love each other, and they're coming along just great.

Laura, we know you're not living the life you had planned for yourself, but please realize that you've far exceeded your own dreams. You're exactly the kind of person we dreamed you'd be, except even more so. But that doesn't mean that you're through! Keep dreaming and keep following your dreams.

You're way too much like me—you worry way too much. The thing I never learned in life was to trust more and worry less. If I had done a better job at my lessons, maybe I could have taught you. I'd probably still be worried about the things I did wrong with you and your sister, but we don't worry here. Maybe you're smarter than I was and you'll learn that on your own. I never became well known or wildly successful, but I look down at you, your sister, and my grandchildren and know that my every dream was fulfilled. I couldn't have wished for more.

Can't wait to see you! Well, yes, I can, and I will wait. Don't hurry through life. Embrace every minute. Sorry I can't talk more about what it's like here, but you know, those things are supposed to be a surprise.

Remember, even though you can't see or feel us, your daddy and I are always with you! And with the kids! Hug those boys for me!

Mom

Apparently, I do know what my mom would say. Maybe we all do.

My mom still writing letters?

REGRETS AND PREMONITIONS

Someone once told me that having regrets was stupid. One should acknowledge mistakes, learn from them, and move forward. Further rumination would be a waste of mental and emotional energy. What a positive, even laudable, approach to life! It is also one that I doubt many of us have mastered. I certainly haven't. I constantly butt my head up against the brick wall of reality and begin wondering "what if" and thinking "if only."

Perhaps the premise itself is flawed. Rumination might simply be part of processing regret. It allows us to learn, to determine to do better next time before letting go of it. Perhaps regretting is an integral part of our growth, nature's way of teaching us those hard lessons in a visceral way. As toddlers, we probably all had some vague understanding that the goal of walking was to stay off the ground. If hitting the ground didn't hurt, however, how much longer would it have taken us to learn to walk upright?

Obviously, little and trivial regrets may not warrant a story. But don't rule out the little things. We all sweat the small stuff. If you put some thought into why a little thing seemed significant and stuck in your craw, you might find a story lurking in the shadows. Perhaps it was something you did unintentionally. Perhaps it's regret over an omission—something left undone or unsaid. What exactly was left unsaid? Was your loved one left with a lack of understanding, or were you denied your last chance to say the things that were already deeply engrained in your relationship? Examining why these incidents still irk you or explaining what the better outcome would have been can help you translate these little things into narratives and meaningful written reflections. Writing these narratives can also help you come to peace with those regrets.

The so-called big stuff—the painful moments or difficult lessons—often stand out because they altered our lives in measureable ways. The other possible outcomes loom over us in huge, dark thunderclouds of

"What if?" The mistakes we've made or think we might have made haunt our sleep as well as our waking thoughts. Though more difficult to share with others than comedic anecdotes, these stories yearn to be written. The mere fact that we continue to ruminate about these instances, often years later, does reveal something about our nature—and not just our propensity to ruminate. These poignant stories of regret are about more than the bumps on the road—they reveal how we felt about our journeys over or around those bumps. Sometimes writing about such instances can help us let go of the regret. Other times, sharing the stories can help others understand and appreciate exactly why we can't let go or how we've channeled our regret into something positive.

Premonitions, on the other hand, are not things that all of us have. Even if we do feel a strong intuition, not all of us listen to it. Though I have experienced feelings that seemed like premonitions, rarely have they ever come true. In my case, these feelings are probably more of a manifestation of my worried subconsciousness or my neuroses.

There are people, though, who are greatly impacted by their experiences with these feelings. My grandmother, staunch Southern Baptist though she was, experienced premonitions from time to time. Writing about them in her Treasure Chest helped her figure out how they fit into her life and events around her. These are some of the most personal writings in her collection, and we appreciate the gift of trust she gave us by writing about them.

Writing about regrets or premonitions can be therapeutic. Your loved ones will certainly benefit from reading about them because what we regret and wonder about are integral parts of who we are. Organizing your thoughts, identifying your feelings, and writing about them can be cathartic and healthy. After you've examined your regrets and premonitions and pondered how they've affected your life, the decision of sharing these writings with your loved ones becomes more straightforward.

Additional Tools:

Worksheet: Identifying Regrets helps you build an idea bank of regrets to write about in your Treasure Chest.

My Turn: Premonition or Not? makes you think about the value of forewarning.

Worksheet: Identifying Regrets

Read over the following questions and jot down some notes. After you've been through the worksheet once, go back through and identify a few topics that you would consider writing about. Fill in the details or, better yet, make an idea bank.

Biggest Regrets

If there were ten things that you could change from your past, which would you choose?

What if it were only one? What would you change?

Was there something you learned through a regret or premonition that you would not have learned otherwise?

Is there a regret that you turned into something positive?

Regrets about People

Did you have any friendships and relationships that kept you away from other activities or passions?

Was there anyone you completely misjudged, for good or for bad?

Were there any people you let down, even if they didn't know it?

Were there any people you hurt?

Were there any people you should have stood up to?

Are there any people with whom you've lost touch?

Spoken Regrets

What do you wish you'd said during times you kept quiet?

What you wish you'd said instead of what you did say?

When you wish you'd kept your peace?

Knowledge

What do you wish you'd known? What would you have done differently with that knowledge?

What do you wish you hadn't asked about (or that you would've been better off not knowing)?

The Road Not Taken

What dreams do you wish you'd pursued?

Which dreams turned out to be illusions or wastes of time?

When was the grass not nearly as green as it appeared?

My Turn: Premonition or Not?

Some refer to premonitions as gifts. Maybe that's so. Surely it would be good to have at least some inkling of events to come so that when the kids come running in and tell you that there's a fire across the street, you're not walking out expecting to roast marshmallows when the fire trucks come screaming up. (That happened.) But is avoiding a total shock worth the dread that a premonition would bring?

When my kids were two and four years old, I had a flat tire while visiting a friend. I discovered the flat as naptime approached, and I was trying to beat a path toward home before my friend, pregnant with her first child, started panicking about her impending motherhood. Naptime was delayed while we went inside, called AAA, waited the requisite forty-five minutes for the truck to show, and let my friend see the boys when they were whiny and irritable. Finally, after AAA put the spare tire on, we headed to the tire store for another wait in less-than-kid-friendly surroundings.

My eldest, then four, climbed up in my lap and looked solemnly at our car on the lift. "Mom, we're having a really unlucky day, aren't we?"

Maybe it *had* been hot in the parking lot watching the AAA man put on the spare, and the tire store was a little loud, dusty, and stinky—but it was hardly a catastrophe. I decided to make it a teaching moment. I gave him a big hug and laughed. I remember telling him, "No, not at all. If this is the worst thing that happens to us today, we'll be doing just fine. This isn't a biggie."

I was right. The flat tire wasn't a biggie. However, those cheerful words have haunted me, for that wasn't to be the worst thing to happen to us that Tuesday afternoon. A biggie loomed in our immediate future. Little could I know that while I was playing the unflappable and cheerful mom in Michigan, my parents, who were vacationing in Alaska, had just died in a fatal car crash.

So, would I like the "gift" of premonition?

Nah, I'd rather bumble around in blissful ignorance.

PRAYERS AND BLESSINGS

Growing up in the Bible Belt, I've seen people who wear their spirituality unabashed; it's as public as their hair color. Living for decades outside of the south, I've seen an equal number of people who regard their spiritual side as one of the most private aspects of themselves. Sometimes, unless we are a person of the cloth or the layman equivalent, we may be hesitant to share our faith or lack thereof, say prayers aloud, or formulate blessings. The fact that my grandmother was willing to reveal her prayers in her writings has always seemed to be an act of great trust. Even if your spirituality isn't based on an organized church or religion, you will still have thoughts of hope and thankfulness, and expressing them will greatly enrich your Treasure Chest. Preserving and sharing your prayers and blessings can be a wonderful gift for your loved ones.

Though the Southern Baptist church of my youth encouraged personal testimonies, I nevertheless regarded them to be a great big, fat, huge, hairy deal—a baring of the soul before strangers. For many, talking or writing about the affairs of their souls amounts to a significant show of intimacy—a daunting degree of self-revelation.

Despite the fact that writing about such topics does not come easily for most of us, the trust and intimacy that is imbued in prayers and blessings can be deeply meaningful for those who read or witness them. I have a great deal of respect for those willing to talk to others about the profound moments of their lives and faith, not just in the traditional church testimony but in everyday life and writing. Recently, while attending a Bar Mitzvah ceremony, I found the blessing the father gave to his son particularly moving. Giving the blessing was not an easy thing for my friend to do in public, but his public profession of his love, hope, and faith for his son touched us all. It is with this respect that I suggest you consider writing about such personal matters. You know yourself and your readers. Would they be honored or moved by the inclusion of such writings in your Treasure Chest?

Consider writing about one of the following:

Prayers of Hope

Any subject is appropriate for this—hope for your family, for the world at large, or for a particular circumstance. Ever have a moment when you felt uplifted? Try capturing it on paper.

Prayers of hope are not only appropriate for happy occasions. We often hope through our worries and worry despite our hopefulness. Prayers of hope can also be written to express exactly in what (or whom) our hope lies.

Prayers of Lament

Lamentations are perhaps our most private prayers. When it comes to sharing our prayers with others, we feel much more comfortable singing praises and expressing gratitude. The human condition, however, is such that we are not apt to respond to grief, divorce, suffering, or other losses with trust and gratitude. In our private moments, we find ourselves asking the perennial "Why?" if not lashing out at God. We wonder if others suffer from doubt and rage. We're hard-pressed to reveal to others that we have moments of doubt and that God sometimes feels very remote and not the least bit in control.

Unquestionably, these moments of anger and doubt in which we converse with God are among our most vulnerable and exposed.

Sharing these tender, poignant, open moments can form strong connections and deepen understanding. It was precisely these writings in my grandmother's Treasure Chest that enabled me to feel connected to her as a woman instead of just a grandmother. As her grief and anger became tangible to me, I gained a much deeper understanding of her faith and hope. It gave me a glimpse of the complete Hazel, as opposed to the grandmother I thought I knew. It also was a testament to the fact that faith can grow out of doubt.

Blessings for Young People

Hope for a child is a common human condition. It resonates deeply. Prayers and blessings for those for whom we hope the hardest are moving not only to the recipients but also to all who share our affection for this young person. For the child involved, the realization that their parents' hopes for them were as strong as or stronger than their hopes for themselves can forge a priceless bond.

Statements of Faith

Young confirmands often write a statement of their faith to share with their congregations as they complete the confirmation process. Likewise, Bar and Bat Mitzvah candidates prepare a Torah section to present. Why not us, then?

Inspiration

Of course, since this writing is in communication with the Creator, it's only logical to lean on scripture, creeds, and traditional writings to find inspiration. In addition, to get a feel for the type of prayer or blessing that you might want to include, looking over traditional or published prayers and blessings can be immensely helpful. You can then decide if you would rather write a "Dear God" kind of letter, a blessing more along the lines of the "May the . . ." Celtic Blessing, or something in between.

Your Turn

You have to know and trust yourself and your readers in this, but I aim to follow my grandmother's example. Her written laments not only pull me closer to her but also give me a boost when I falter in my own faith. Her prayers of hope and faith inspire me as I follow her example in writing about my faith. I'm not sure that I'll produce truly inspirational material, but I am confident that I will connect with others. Now it's your turn, if you choose to take it.

Additional Tools:

Worksheet: Idea Bank for Prayers helps you develop ideas of prayers to compose.

Worksheet: Writing Blessings for Loved Ones guides you as you write a blessing for a loved one.

My Turn: Prayer for a Young Man's Back is my own prayer for my son.

Worksheet: Idea Bank for Prayers

There are countless times and circumstances that inspire us to pray. As you look through the below list, mark those that appeal to you with short notes.

Times of Happiness and Gratitude

- Falling in love:

- Engagement:

- Marriage:

- Graduation:

- Starting college:

- Starting grad school:

- Receiving a degree:

- Starting a career:

- Positive career move:

- New job:

- New home:

- Safe travels:

- Pride in children:

- Just having a great day:

- Religious holidays:

- Personal milestones:

- Prosperity:

- Feeling hopeful:

- Simple gratitude:

- Relief:

- Dodging a bullet:

- Birth of a child:

- New friends:

- Inspiration from nature:

- Good health:

- Restored health:

- Restored relationships:

- Small moments:

- Dream fulfilled:

Introspective Times

- Making a decision:

- Life changes:

- Family changes:

- Contemplating family changes:

- A child leaving home:

- Religious celebrations:

- Religious sacraments:

- Disappointed in others:

- Compassion or empathy for others:

- Disappointed by life:

- Facing fears or anxieties:

- Standing up for what is right:

- Being in the minority:

- Discerning or figuring out what is right:

- Coming to a new understanding:

- Contemplating the future:

- Contemplating the past:

- Searching for balance in life:

- Trying to accept something:

- Pondering:

- Wondering why:

- Wondering if or what if:

- Preparing yourself:

- Prayers of confession:

- Prayers for the world:

- Interfaith prayers:

- Prayers for wisdom or clarity:

- Prayers for peace of mind:

- Prayers for strength:

- Prayers for forgiveness:

- Prayers for simplicity:

- Figuring out whether to speak out or keep silent:

Difficult Times

- Losing a loved one:

- Marriage trouble:

- Rocky Relationship:

- Difficulties with kids:

- Kids facing difficulties:

- Single parenthood:

- Crisis of faith:

- Health problems:

- Mental health issues:

- Career or job problems:

- Loss of job or income:

- Broken friendship:

- Betrayal:

- Rejection:

- Abandonment:

- Hurt feelings:

- Righteous indignation:

- Inability to forgive:

- Guilt:

- Bad things happening to good people:

- Losing your optimism for the future:

- Difficulties with fertility or adoption:

- Injustice:

- Feeling hopeless

- Dealing with hatred or bitterness

- Letting go of hatred or bitterness:

- Tragedy in the community:

Statements of Faith

- Confessing what you believe:

- Admitting your doubts:

- Prayers concerning your own unbelief:

- Expressions of faith:

- Growing closer to God:

- Prayers of commitment:

Worksheet: Writing Blessings for Loved Ones

For: _____ (Name of loved one)

Occasions

Is there a special occasion or event that has inspired this writing?

Did a spiritual celebration inspire this blessing? (Shabbat blessing, naming, baptism, confirmation, bar mitzvah, or similar events)

Are there other special circumstances that prompted this writing, such as the health or mental health of the writer or the subject? Consider whether knowing these circumstances will enrich your readers' understanding of your piece and whether it's too personal or private to include.

At what phase of life (baby, child, youth, young adult, newlywed, retiree, and so on) is this person? Find a way to work that into your writing so that the reader has a sense of it.

Is the subject of your prayer or blessing facing a major life transition?

What?

What blessings does this person already possess?

What hardships does this person face in the future?

What challenges does this person currently have?

What do you dream for this person's future?

What qualities does this person have that will be helpful in facing the future?

What role does your loved one's personal faith have in this prayer?

Other Considerations

Do you want to include references to or claim promises from your Bible or other holy book?

Do you want or need to mention other people in this prayer, like siblings, spouses, children, or parents?

If so, in what way do these other people influence your subject's prospects for happiness? What do you hope for their continued relationship?

My Turn: Prayer for a Young Man's Back

Of late I mostly see him coming and going—to and from school, practice, games, or work—so I see as much of his back as his face. The sight of him leaving causes me to screw up my courage a little. Soon he'll be off on his own. Then I'll have to screw up my courage a lot.

As I watch his back, I pray for it.

I pray
that the Lord God watch it for me,
when I can't be there to do it,
and even when I can.

that it will be resilient enough
    to bear life's storms without
    breaking
that it will be flexible enough to
    take him into new adventures,
    even if he has to stretch
that it will be embraced by many
    a friend
that these same friends and loved
    ones will have his back when
    it matters
that it will be true enough to pull
    him back to those things he
    loves

"I see as much of his back as his face."

that he give it adequate rest and care
that it will be strong enough to bear the loads he's destined to carry,
    and
that it won't bear too much of a load
that he'll share it with others—
God, parents, family, church, friends

that its strength will help and inspire others
that it will be warmed with the sun, (my personal metaphor for all the
    "fun" he's planning to have), without burning
that he'll wear sun screen (another mother's metaphor).

that I'll see it less than I see his smile.

OTHER REFLECTIONS

Not everything fits into a nice, neat little category—nor should it. Likewise, this guide isn't an exhaustive summary of all the things you might possibly want to include in your personal legacy—it's merely a starting point. As mentioned in the Other Writings section earlier, you might already have writings on hand that you want to include. You might have philosophical stances that you would like to explain or an outlook on the world that is different from others'. If you are living with a chronic or emotional illness, you might want to write a "day in the life" type of reflection or treat the subject in a different way. It might be an emotional bucket list or a list of the places you'd like to see in your life.

Continue to reflect on your memories, values, and moral code, and see if there is anything else that moves you to write. Not everything has to be for public consumption. Go ahead and try writing about some of these topics. Read the finished product. If it isn't baring the soul too much, include it in your Treasure Chest.

Additional Tools:

Worksheet: Keep Reflecting supplies prompts for other reflections to pack in your Treasure Chest.

Worksheet: Keep Reflecting

Keep reflecting about the things that define you and try to put them into writing. In addition to the items mentioned in the text (philosophical stances, world views, days in your life, bucket lists), try some of these:

Experiences that shaped me:

What I would change about myself if I could:

The one thing I would never change about myself:

When I was happiest or most uplifted:

What it felt like:

Why I was happy:

How long it lasted:

In dark, stressful, and sorrowful times, what pulled me through:

Who and where I drew strength from:

Who and where I drew hope from:

Who I drew companionship and support from:

The loves in my life:

Why I love them:

Why they love me:

Why we're good for each other:

Part 5

Final Considerations

WHEN TO STOP

Just as there are no right or wrong ways of constructing your Treasure Chest, by extension, there are no right or wrong ways of ending it.

The term *Treasure Chest* carries with it the connotation of buried or sunken treasure that waits in obscurity until the dogged explorer finds it after decades of searching. By implication, treasures are stored away in their entirety until the booty, in all its bountiful glory, is revealed and shared.

When you weigh how you want to reveal and end your Treasure Chest, be aware that one event does not have to precede the other. You can reveal your in-progress Treasure Chest without ending it for decades to come. The opposite is also true. No one needs to see your work until you feel that it is (or you are) ready.

One obvious option is to wait to reveal your Treasure Chest until you deem it full or finished. You can write in secret and share your final product with whatever degree of pomp and circumstance suits you. My grandmother revealed her Treasure Chest as she faced the end stage of her battle with cancer. I personally think she did not so much finish it as she ran out of time to write in it. Though it was a surprise, it came with little fanfare. This was the only method with which my grandmother was comfortable. Not unlike a literal treasure, it was her bequest to pass on to her loved ones.

There are other ways of looking at a Treasure Chest, however. Treasure chests of old were often simply repositories for treasures, places of relative security in which to store valued objects. I imagine that most of these treasure chests were not kept with the expectation of opening them only once, on the day the horde was handed over to relatives. It was a chest for the safekeeping of precious gems and heirlooms. Doubtlessly, most treasure chests were opened on those occasions when the owner wished to riffle through them and admire or contemplate the items within.

Likewise, your Treasure Chest isn't necessarily destined to be turned over to someone else's ownership and control at a particular date or time in your life. It can simply be a place in which you store, process, muse over, and reflect upon your memories. Unlike a physical chest, your Treasure Chest has no finite space limitations. You can store as many or as few things in it as you want. You can open and share the contents of your Treasure Chest regardless of the number of memories and stories it holds. There may be great enjoyment in store for you as you invite loved ones to take a peak, riffle through, and gaze at your trinkets and gems.

If you are crafting your legacy of memories with a target date or event in mind, you might prefer to work quietly until you feel you've included those memories most crucial to you. That doesn't mean you have to stop writing when the target date has come and gone.

Yet another way to look at your Treasure Chest is to consider it more of a chest for blankets and other things that warm you and your loved ones on chilly evenings. It can contain small coverlets you want to lend out as well big, warm quilts under which you snuggle up to those closest to you. You can share your legacy of memories as a finished product or as a dynamic document—a perpetual work in progress.

There's no right time to stop writing. Your writing may feel like a pilgrimage of sorts, and you may come to a point where you feel that you've reached the end of your journey. On the other hand, the exercise of writing might be more analogous to a restaurant you like to frequent, feasting on the things you enjoy with the people that matter to you. You may be more of a collector of memories, and like many collectors, you might never stop collecting—you may just grow more discriminating in the items you add to your collection.

How and when you choose to conclude your writing (or volumes of writings) is limited only by your creativity and personal preferences.

THE BIG (OR LITTLE) REVEAL

Wouldn't it be great if life was just like an episode of *Extreme Home Makeover*? We'd identify a project and then go off on vacation while hundreds of qualified professionals completed it beyond our most optimistic expectations. We'd skip the tours of the work in progress and never have to say to friends, "Well, it's not finished, but what we were thinking is . . ." Instead, we'd arrive in town to a cheering crowd, someone would yell, "Move that bus!" and as the behemoth that was blocking the view slowly rolled away, the finished project would stand in shining perfection.

Alas, it's not like that. A Treasure Chest reveal is more complicated. First of all, it's a labor of love, so it wouldn't be the same if someone else did it for you—even if that someone was a big crowd of experts. Additionally, a house presents itself by simply existing, but there are tons of options for presenting a work of writing. Let's examine those complexities and the options they give you before you decide on your method of revelation.

Packaging

First, ask yourself what you want people to see when that figurative bus drives away. My grandmother presented us with a journal that was barely legible. After my mom transcribed and typed her writings, she made copies and presented them to us each in a simple red paper folder. The humble presentation didn't decrease the value of the gift in the slightest. My mother and grandmother clearly understood that the gift was in the contents, not the packaging. That said, I must admit that it wouldn't be my choice. But then, I'm fairly compulsive about wrapping and presenting gifts.

Again, there is no right way to present your Treasure Chest. There is simply what you choose. In keeping with your personality, creativity, health, and life circumstances, you can choose from a whole gambit of packaging. Do you want it printed? Bound? You could go all the way and present it in scrapbook form. If you're going the digital route, do you want to burn your memories onto discs or make yourself a website? Do you want to upload them, one at a time, to a blog? (See Recommended Resources for more ideas.)

Finished Product—or Not

As we discussed in When to Stop, consider whether you're sharing a work in progress or a finished edition of your Treasure Chest. One advantage of presenting a work in progress is that you don't have to wait until you've told all your stories before you start sharing.

If you prefer to start dialogs with family members by sharing a dynamic, growing Treasure Chest, you can start sharing your memories on a piecemeal basis. If you're technologically adventurous, blogging offers a huge advantage—your readers can comment immediately and respond to one another.

Whom to Invite

You can make your blog or website as public or as private as you'd like. Deciding exactly whom you want to invite to the big reveal party isn't always easy. If you were working towards a concrete time or event, it's a little easier. If you've been open about your endeavor, you may have friends and relatives chomping at the bit to see your work. If you haven't told anyone what you're working on, you might have to do a little upfront advertising or unveil it to a few people on an individual basis. Do you want to have people let you know if they're interested, or do you just want to self-publish and deliver a finished Treasure Chest to each of them?

Letting Go

There are perfectionists that have trouble letting go of a project that is basically complete. As a writer, I can relate to this. This isn't a new issue; it's the reason there are so many Chicken Soup for the Soul books. Having a reveal doesn't mean you can't continue to write. There are always second editions and serials. If you've reached a logical stopping point, don't delay the big reveal for one additional entry.

Bon Voyage

I wish you much joy and adventure on your journey of collecting your memories and stories. Refer to http://www.treasurechestofmemories.com for ongoing tips and ideas.

RECOMMENDED
RESOURCES

Books on Writing Better:

The following three books are the ultimate guides for writing and style:

William Strunk and E.B. White, *The Elements of Style, 4ᵗʰ Edition.* Longman, 1999.

William Zinsser, *On Writing Well, 30th Anniversary Edition: An Informal Guide to Writing Nonfiction,* Harper, 2012.

William Zinsser, *Writing About Your Life,* Marlow, 2004.

Internet Resources and Articles

Mignon Fogerty, "Grammar Girl—Quick and Dirty Tips," http://www.quickanddirty-tips.com/grammar-girl. This comprehensive site has searchable archives of tips on grammar, punctuation, and word usage.

Ned Hickman, "Tips to jump-start your writing (unless you're in Arkansas). http://ned-hickson.wordpress.com/2013/06/21/tips-to-jump-start-your-writing-unless-youre-in-arkansas/. This article supplies a humorist's take on breaking through writer's blocks.

Nischala Murthy, "12 Most Compelling Reasons for You to Write." *12most.com,* http://12most.com/2011/11/22/12-compelling-reasons-write/. This article provides inspiration when you need it most.

Jessica Strawser, "9 Ways to Get Started & Stay Motivated." *Writer's Digest.* July 09, 2010. http://www.writersdigest.com/article/ 9-ways-to-get-started-and-stay-moti-vated/. This post gives helpful advice on staying on task.

Vonnegut, Kurt. "How to Write With Style." [excerpt from: How to Use the Power of the Printed Word, Doubleday.] *Peterstekel.com,* http://peterstekel.com/PDF-HTML/Kurt%20Vonnegut%20advice%20to%20writers.htm. This is a practical and concise guide to writing better.

William Zinsser, "On Memoir, Truth, and 'Writing Well:' NPR Interview with William Zinsser, author of On Writing Well," Airdate April 13, 2006, http://www.npr.org/

templates/story/story.php?storyId=5340618. This interview contains valuable insight about writing about your life.

On Writing (Better) about Your Past

Matilda Butler and Kendra Bonnett (Editors), Seasons of our Lives series. Each book of these four books presents memories from various writers, each followed by an assessment of the writing techniques used.

Typography and Font Selection

"What's the Best Font For Websites and Blogs?", Integral Web Solutions, April 2, 2011, http://www.integralwebsolutions.co.za/Blog/EntryId/832/Whats-The-Best-Font-For-Websites-and-Blogs.aspx.

Douglas Bonneville, "How to Choose a Typeface," Smashing Magazine, March 24, 2011, http://www.smashingmagazine.com/2011/03/24/how-to-choose-a-typeface/.

Using Colors for Contast

Kasper Aaberg, Color Contrast--all about the difference," Love of Graphicsm http://www.loveofgraphics.com/graphicdesign/color/colorcontrast/. This article presents an overview of contrasting colors and makes some basic recommendations.

Genealogy Resources

"Preserving Family Treasures & Heirlooms: How to Protect and Save Them for Future Generations" by Kimberly Powell gives down to earth advise about displaying, inventorying, and preserving family treasures. Published online by About.com at http://genealogy.about.com/library/weekly/aa_preserving_heirlooms.htm.

Blogging Resources

The best blogging resources are online. Many print books on the market are geared towards those wanting to blog for income. If any of these links no longer work, use your search engine. Help is only a few keystrokes away.

"Top 10 Blog Websites to Create Free Blogs," by Top Sites Blog, can be found at http://topsitesblog.com/blog-websites/ or by entering "Top 10 Blog Websites Top Sites Blog" into the search engine of your choice. Each blog site discussed (and linked) has a getting started page.

Blogging for Dummies, by Susannah Gardner and Shane Birley, published by John Wiley and Sons, Inc., Hoboken NJ, in 2012.

Blog Websites' Getting Started Guides:

Blogger.com's Blogger Tour can be accessed at https://www.blogger.com/tour_start.g.
Wordpress's home page has options for getting started: www.wordpress.com.
Blog.com likewise helps visitors get started right from the homepage: www.blog.com

Scrapbooking Your Memories

Beyond the Branches: Writing and Scrapping Your Personal Family Tree by Robyn Conley, published by Roots and Branches in 2007, ISBN-10: 0937660248. This is a guide to making a family history scrapbook.

Soliciting Materials from Relatives

Reminiscing Board Game, by Reminiscing Game, is a game for "people over thirty." Available at vendors such as Amazon or SeniorStore.com, you're armed for good fun and the potential for an onslaught memories coming to the surface.

Books on Interviewing Relatives

Bob Greene and D.G. Fulford, *To Our Children's Children: Preserving Family Histories for Generations to Come.* Doubleday, 1993. ISBN-10: 0385467971. A useful guide to creating a personal history of older family members for future generations.

Cynthia Hart and Lisa Samson, *The Oral History Workshop: Collect and Celebrate the Life Stories of Your Family and Friends.* Workman Publishing, 2009. ISBN-10: 0761151974. Provides an in depth guide to preparing for and conducting interviews and how to assimilate the narratives into scrap-book or narrative interviewing relatives.

Internet Resources on Interviewing Relatives:

Lynn Palmero, "7 Tools for your next Family History Interview," http://www.thearmchairgenealogist.com/2013/06/7-tools-for-your-next-family-history.html. Lynn also offers a free e-book, *The Complete Guide to the Family History Interview: 130 Questions.*

"10 Tips for Interviewing Family Members," http://blog.myheritage.com/2013/06/10-tips-for-interviewing-family-members-2/?utm_source=feedburner&utm_medium=feed&utm_campaign=Feed:+MyheritageBlog+%28MyHeritage+Blog%29&utm_content=Google+Reader,

Colloquial and Regional Expressions:

"AmeriSpeak." http://goodlingos.com/ or enter "AmeriSpeak" in your search engine. This site has an exhaustive list of categories of colloquial and regional expressions. You can find funny or dumb expressions or explore by subject.

ABOUT THE AUTHOR

LAURA HEDGECOCK was born in South Carolina but came to live in Michigan by way of Chicago and Germany. Leaving her career in international business to be a stay-at-home mom as well as her association with non-profits led her to help others tell their stories. *Memories of Me: A Complete Guide to Telling and Sharing the Stories of Your Life* results from the intersection of Ms. Hedgecock's experiences in genealogy, photography, and scrapbooking, as well her journey of compiling her own memories. She blogs about preserving and sharing memories at http://www. TreasureChestofMemories.com.